The Archaeology of Mesoamerica

The Archaeology of Mesoamerica

Mexican and European Perspectives

Editors: Warwick Bray and Linda Manzanilla
with the editorial collaboration of Clara Bezanilla

Published for The Trustees of

The British Museum by

BRITISH MUSEUM PRESS

© 1999 The Trustees of the British Museum

Published by British Museum Press
A division of The British Museum Company Ltd
46 Bloomsbury Street, London WC1B 3QQ

A catalogue record for this book is available from the British Library

ISBN 0–7141–2529–6

Designed and typeset in Sabon by John Hawkins Book Design
Printed in Great Britain by Cambridge University Press

Contents

Foreword: Mexico in the British Museum

This book emerged from an international collaboration between Mexico and the United Kingdom that led in 1994 to the creation of the new Mexican Gallery in the British Museum. The gallery was designed by a leading Mexican architect, Teodoro González de León, and the successful outcome was the fruit of a determined combined effort involving Ethnography Department curators, British Museum Design Office staff and colleagues from the Consejo Nacional para la Cultura y las Artes and from the Instituto Nacional de Antropología e Historia. To celebrate the opening of the gallery, a scholars' conference entitled 'Mesoamerican Studies: Mexican and European Perspectives' took place in February 1995. For publication we have retained the subtitle of that meeting, since this volume embodies the wider scholarly exchange that marked the spirit of the conference itself.

The essays in the book were originally delivered as conference papers. Contributors were asked to reflect upon the implications of the excavations, fieldwork or historical investigations they had conducted during the past decade, and to do so in whatever way they thought best for a mixed audience of professionals and serious amateurs. The intention was not to provide yet another collection of journal-style papers. Instead, the aim was to offer a broad mixture of up-to-date syntheses (bringing the most recent work of Mexican scholars to a wider, English-speaking audience) together with more detailed studies emphasizing some of the different ways of looking at indigenous Mexico, past and present. These distinctive approaches are, inevitably, as diverse as the personalities of the authors themselves. In a two-day meeting it was clearly impossible to cover the whole of Mexican archaeology, but we hope this 'memorial volume' will bring back memories for those who were there and, at a time when textbooks quickly go out of date, provide current and reliable information for anyone interested in ancient Mexico.

Exhibits in the Mexican Gallery at the British Museum with the Fire Serpent, Xiuhcoatl (Aztec AD 1300–1521), in the foreground. (Photo © British Museum)

This volume also implicitly calls attention to a wider, and as yet unfulfilled, obligation to undertake comprehensive and systematic study of the full range and depth of the Museum's Mexican collections. The objects displayed in the gallery form only a part of the permanent collections of the British Museum, most acquired during the large expansion in its holdings during the nineteenth century. The accompanying publication, *Ancient Mexico in the British Museum* by

Colin McEwan (British Museum Press, 1994), was specifically tailored to the gallery installation and intended to serve as an introductory guide to a broad audience of international visitors to the Museum. The larger task of promoting scholarly research into the collections has only just begun in earnest. Progress has already been made with a pilot study being conducted by Peter Mathews on the unique collection of plaster casts of Maya sculpture made by Alfred Maudslay well over a century ago. These preserve a wealth of information that has in many cases been lost on the original monuments due to weathering and looting. We anticipate that the results of this study, together with archival research being conducted by Robert Aguirre, will complement Ian Graham's forthcoming biography of Maudslay currently in

Lintel 25 (Maya, c.AD 725) from Yaxchilán in the Mexican Gallery, British Museum, showing the spirit of a warrior, perhaps a deified ancestor, emerging from the jaws of a double-headed serpent above Lady Xok (the ruler's wife), who is holding ritual blood-letting instruments.

preparation. Together these will be incorporated into the 'Archaeology in Action' programme which is being planned for the new
British Museum Study Centre.

In a parallel initiative a significant collection of Pre-Columbian
sculpture from Mexico assembled in the early nineteenth century by
William Bullock will feature in the Museum's online COMPASS
project. Plans are also underway to develop a computer animation of
the Codex Zouche-Nuttall to bring the dynastic histories of twelfth-
century Mixtec lords to life for specialists and students alike.

These and future projects will, we hope, pave the way for continued
reciprocal exchanges of ideas, resources and scholars, and will help
make the Museum's collection accessible to study and interpretation
in ways hitherto undreamt of. Activities of this kind will necessitate
international cooperation and enlightened sponsorship, as will
indispensable longer-term goals, including the creation of a gallery
devoted exclusively to the Museum's outstanding Maya collections.
The generous collaborative spirit that gave rise to the scholars'
conference will be required in even greater measure if these hopes are
to be realized.

Acknowledgements

Funding for the 1995 scholars' conference came from the former
Baring Foundation whose then Director, David Carrington, strongly
supported our educational initiatives to make the cultures of Mexico
better known and to seek to link European and Mexican scholarship
in a substantive and sustained way. This support enabled us to bring
together some of the leading researchers among the new generation of
Mexican archaeologists, and we are most grateful to them for their
presence at the conference and for their much valued contributions to
this volume which grew out of it. We would also like to thank warmly
Dr Felipe Solis Olguín of the Museo Nacional de Antropología,
Mexico City, and Otto Schondube of the Museo Regional de
Guadalajara for their participation in the conference itself.

Penny Bateman of the Education Department and Norma Rosso,
Special Assistant in the Ethnography Department, handled the
arrangements for the conference most effectively, and the convivial
and constructive nature of the gathering was due in no small measure
to their unstinting efforts.

Finally, we would like to record our gratitude to those who have worked on this book. The Museum itself is indebted to our joint editors, Warwick Bray and Linda Manzanilla, for their hard work in pulling the volume together. Within the Department of Ethnography, Clara Bezanilla deserves special mention for her tireless work in co-ordinating and checking texts and liaising between editors, authors and our publishers. Within British Museum Press, Emma Way and especially Carolyn Jones have, as always, been thoroughly supportive. Thanks are also due to Haydn Kirnon for translating 'Water and Fire: Archaeology in the Capital of the Mexica Empire' by Leonardo López Luján and to Isabel Anderton for translating 'The Gulf Coast Cultures and the Recent Archaeological Discoveries at El Manatí, Veracruz' by Ponciano Ortíz Ceballos and Ma. del Carmen Rodríguez Martínez.

At the time this volume was in the final stages of preparation the death was announced of Dr Linda Schele. Dr Schele took a leading part in a ground-breaking workshop on Maya epigraphy held at the British Museum, also in 1995. This book is respectfully dedicated to her memory to add a Mexican and European perspective to the tributes paid to her by her colleagues in the United States.

John Mack, Keeper of the Department of Ethnography
Colin McEwan, Assistant Keeper and Curator for Central and South America

1. The First Urban Developments in the Central Highlands of Mesoamerica

Linda Manzanilla

The nature of the Mesoamerican city

Life in urban centres and cities was a characteristic of civilization in Mesoamerica and Mesopotamia. In spite of differences in form and function (Marcus 1983), the majority of the Mesoamerican cities included civic, administrative and ceremonial cores, and also huge demographic concentrations that offered goods and services to the productive surrounding territories.

Yet there was a difference between the urban centres in the central Mexican highlands and those of the Maya area. This difference lay in the importance assigned to craft production and specialization within the core itself, and in the integration of foreign groups into urban life. According to Freidel (1981), in cities of the Basin of Mexico, such as Teotihuacan, the main goal of large-scale nucleation was the control of people, whereas the main goal of residential dispersion in the Maya area was the control of the distribution of goods and services.

The Classic period of Mesoamerica occupies the first nine centuries AD. During this period a new way of life which we can call 'urban' developed, and it was also a time of regional integration. There were various aspects that differentiated this period from the succeeding one (the Postclassic): one of these was the overall importance of the temple, not only as a ritual institution but also as an economic sphere controlling production, redistribution, and long distance exchange networks; another was the appearance of specialized crafts.

Beyond any doubt, the city of Teotihuacan exemplified the Classic period in central Mexico. The prehispanic cities of the central highlands were multiethnic centres that took advantage of the occupational specialities of foreign groups; they were also strategic sites with respect to resource disposability, the loci of huge demographic concentrations, the capitals of large states, important manufacturing and exchange centres, and planned settlements laid out according to astronomical standards or ritual axes (Tichy 1983).

Teotihuacan was also a model of this cosmic planning, having a terrestrial sacred space, a synthesis of the four directions of the cosmos which were represented in the four divisions of the city (col. pl. 1), a celestial sphere represented by the summits of the temples and the sky itself, and an Underworld represented by a system of tunnels under the settlement (Manzanilla 1994a, 1994b; Manzanilla *et al.* 1994). It was the place where sacred time was created, as was recently proposed for the Temple of Quetzalcóatl by López Austin, López Luján and Sugiyama (1991). It was thus the archetype of the Mesoamerican civilized city, the most sacred realm, and the mythic Tollan where crafts flourished. It inaugurated a new era in the settlement pattern of the region – an era that has not yet ended.

This essay will review new data derived from my two projects at Teotihuacan: one dealing with the study of domestic life and the other with the Underworld of the ancient site.

1 *An early photograph of the Ciudadela.*

Teotihuacan

Teotihuacan was one of the largest and most important urban developments of pre-industrial times, the main pilgrimage and manufacturing centre of the Classic Period. Its main features are discussed below.

A strategic site

The location of Teotihuacan was chosen for its close proximity to the Otumba and Pachuca obsidian deposits, the fresh-water springs of Puxtla at San Juan, and the Texcoco Lake, and for its privileged position on the easiest access route from the Gulf Coast to the Basin of Mexico. Nevertheless, the location of the first urban centre in the northwestern part of the valley is surprising, because apart from the springs the sector lacks running water. Perhaps the availability of building material was the attraction.

Great demographic concentration

As a result of the eruption of the Xitle volcano in the southwestern portion of the Basin of Mexico, Cuicuilco – one of the largest Formative centres – was abandoned. The Popocatépetl volcano may also have erupted in the Late Formative, as recent data from the site of Tetimpa, buried by the Popo ashes and lapilli, suggests (Uruñuela y Ladrón de Guevara and Plunket Nagoda 1995). The consequent demographic rearrangements provoked massive migrations to the northern part of the Basin of Mexico. Yet one of the possible phenomena associated with the early history of Teotihuacan was the reallocation of population and its channelling to huge constructional enterprises such as the Sun and the Moon Pyramids.

From then on, Teotihuacan was the main settlement of central Mexico, with the rest of the region becoming ruralized. Within the city was concentrated around half of the population of the Basin of Mexico and it was devoted mainly to craft production (Sanders, Parsons and Santley 1979). We can assume that the valleys of Toluca, Tlaxcala and eastern Morelos were dependent on Teotihuacan, and were probably sending cotton, avocados, Thin Orange wares and other products to the city.

Monumentality

As already mentioned, the first urban centre of the Teotihuacan Valley was located in the northwestern sector. It was characterized by three-temple plazas surrounded by the dwellings of the inhabitants. After some time came the construction of the Pyramids of the Sun and Moon, and soon after that, during the first centuries AD, the 'Street of the Dead' was planned, as was the orthogonal grid of the city. The population formerly living in the northwestern sector moved to the fringes of the main avenue, and the city grew steadily until it reached 20 square kilometres (Millon 1973).

The monumentality of the constructions was a major investment in the ideological importance of the settlement. It was the creation of sacred space, as well as sacred time, as represented in the building of the Temple of Quetzalcóatl (López Austin, López Luján and Sugiyama 1991). Millon (1993: 25) believes that the constructions of the Pyramids of the Sun and the Moon, the Ciudadela (fig. 1), and the Street of the Dead are 'dramatic demonstrations, dramatic realizations of the exercise of power during a time of strong rulers'.

Urban planning

Elements of both urban planning at Teotihuacan and domestic life in apartment compounds are clearly defined for the Tlamimilolpa phase (second and third centuries AD), although not before that time (Millon 1973). These elements include:
1. The existence of streets and axes as part of an orthogonal grid oriented to 15° east of astronomical north (see col. pl. 1). This was traced by the use of circular markers in the nearby hills and in the city itself (Aveni, Hartung and Buckingham 1978). Millon proposes the existence of two axes, the Street of the Dead and the East–West Avenue, which divide the city in four quadrants. Tichy (1983) adds that this orientation is linked to the beginnings of the rainy season in May, creating a radial system of visual lines relative to the sun's position on the horizon. The centre of the system was the Pyramid of the Sun.
2. The presence of a water supply and drainage system.
3. Administrative and public constructions placed along the Street of the Dead. The rest of the city was built around three-temple plazas which could have been the centres of wards (*barrios*).
4. The existence of craftsmen's and foreign barrios. Around the main core of the city there were a number of multifamily apartment compounds that consisted of several rooms at slightly different levels, disposed around open spaces such as courtyards, backyards and light wells, these last being places for ritual, rainwater collection, partial rubbish disposal and provision of light. The apartments were provided with corridors and passages; they had domestic sanctuaries and the entire structure was enclosed within an exterior wall.

It is believed that these compounds may have been occupied by corporate groups sharing kinship, residence and occupation, for it has been archaeologically observed that craftsmen dedicated to the manufacture of different products lived in separate compounds (Spence 1966; Millon 1968), though little evidence has yet been published on this topic. However, life in multifamily apartment compounds was a characteristic of urban Teotihuacan and warrants further analysis.

Some of the apartment compounds in the central area of the city have been excavated, among them Tlamimilolpa (fig. 2), Xolalpan,

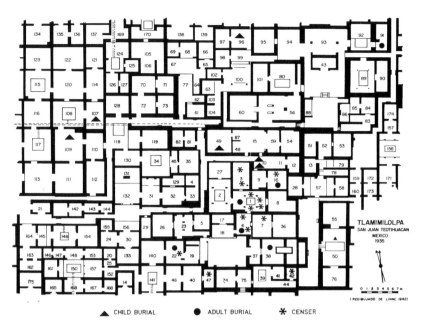

▲ CHILD BURIAL   ● ADULT BURIAL   ✳ CENSER

2 *Map of the Tlamimilolpa apartment compound, excavated by Linné (1942).*

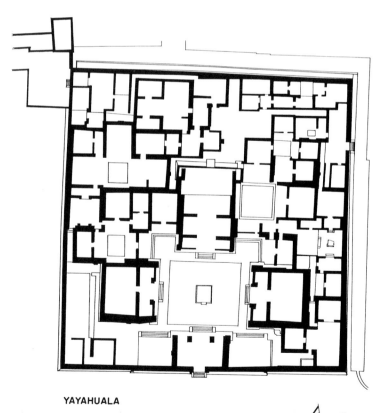

YAYAHUALA

3 *Map of the Yayahuala apartment compound, excavated by Séjourné (1966).*

4 *Aerial view of the Oztoyahualco N6W3 compound.* (Photo: Linda Manzanilla)

Atetelco, Tepantitla, La Ventilla, Tetitla, Zacuala, Yayahuala (fig. 3), Bidasoa, San Antonio Las Palmas, El Cuartel, and structure N6W3:19 at Oztoyahualco. We also have information from Tlajinga 33 (Storey and Widmer 1989; Storey 1992) and Maquixco on the outskirts of the city.

From 1985 to 1988 we carefully dissected an apartment compound at Oztoyahualco (fig. 4), on the northwestern boundary of the city (Barba *et al.* 1987; Manzanilla 1988–9; Manzanilla and Barba 1990; Manzanilla 1993). We knew that the stucco floors were scrupulously swept, so we could not expect to find an abundance of macroscopical remains for our analysis. We thus planned a strategy that looked for chemical traces of activities on the plastered floors, as well as microscopic evidence related to such activities.

The compounds varied considerably in surface area. Apartments within each compound could be identified either by looking at the circulation alleys or access points, or by mapping the different food consumption loci for each nuclear family. In the compound at Oztoyahualco (as in the others) each nuclear family apartment included a zone for food preparation and consumption, sleeping quarters, storage areas, sectors for refuse, patios for cult activities, and funerary areas, and there were zones in which the entire family group gathered to share activities, particularly those related to ritual and perhaps to the raising of domestic animals.

There were occupational differences between domestic units, with activities including lapidary work, ceramic manufacture, obsidian biface production and prismatic blade extraction, figurine production, textile manufacture, probably basket making, hide and fibre work, mural painting and stucco polishing. We suspect that different families participated in such specialized activities. In the compound that we studied, the family group probably specialized in the stucco finishing of neighbouring three-temple plazas and perhaps other structures at Oztoyahualco. Other family groups were devoted to ceramic and textile activities, obsidian working and painting.

With respect to diet, the Mesoamerican plant complex was present in our compound as well as in others – maize, amaranth, beans, squash, hot peppers, tomatoes, cacti, Mexican hawthorn and Mexican cherries. Some medicinal plants were present – particularly white sapodilla and wild potatoes – and probably some colourful flowers (McClung 1979, 1980: 162–3; Manzanilla 1985, 1988–9, 1993; Storey 1992: 64).

The presence of tobacco at San Antonio Las Palmas, avocado at Teopancazco and cotton and related plants at Tlamimilolpa, Teopancazco, Tetitla and Tlajinga 33 suggests differential access to certain botanical resources associated with manufacturing processes and ritual consumption (Linné 1942; McClung 1979; Storey and Widmer 1989; Monzón 1989). Plant species were generally gathered for food, medicinal purposes, fuel and construction. In addition to those already mentioned, purslane, wild reeds, umbelliferous plants, pine, oak, juniper, reeds and bulrushes have been found.

Animal protein was obtained from rabbits and hares, deer, dogs and turkey, supplemented by duck and fish (Starbuck 1975; Valadez and Manzanilla 1988; Valadez Azúa 1993). In Xolalpan times (around AD 550), there may have been shortages of meat as a consequence of population pressure. Perhaps one of the responses to this was the breeding of rabbits, together with turkeys and dogs at Oztoyahualco. Another could have been the consumption of freshwater fish at Tlajinga 33.

Burials were frequent in domestic contexts. However, with the exception of Tlajinga 33 and probably La Ventilla, the number of adults interred in each one of the compounds is too low, relative to the area of the compound, to account for most of its inhabitants. Other adults, particularly women, may have been buried in other places.

Certain burials in each compound had very rich offerings. At Oztoyahualco, Burial 8 was exceptional, containing a twenty-two-year-old male with an intentionally deformed skull, and an impressive theatre-type incense burner (Manzanilla and Carreón 1991). In what seems to represent a funerary ritual, the incense burner appliqués had been removed from the lid and placed around the deceased (col. pl. 2). The 'chimney' of the burner was placed to the west of the skull; the lid and figure to the east; representations of plants and sustenance (ears of corn, squash, squash flowers, cotton, cooked corn, corn bread and perhaps amaranth bread) to the south; and four-petalled flowers, roundels representing feathers and mica discs also to the east and west.

The presence of foreign raw materials such as mica, slate and marine shells in burials at Xolalpan, Tlamimilolpa, and Oztoyahualco should also be mentioned. There were differences between the compounds in the quantities of exotic goods and in the proportion of Pacific versus Atlantic shell species.

Turning to domestic cult, it has been proposed that a two-level hierarchy of deities was present for the first time at Teotihuacan. Lineage gods were patrons of lines of descent, and above them was the deity Tláloc as god of place, protector of the territory and patron of the city and the caves (López Austin 1989). Among the deities present at Teotihuacan, the Fire God (Huehuetéotl), who was known from the Formative Period, always appeared associated with the eastern portions of apartment compounds. Another deity present in domestic contexts was the Fat God, generally represented in figurines or appliquéd on tripod vessels. The Butterfly God was present on incense burners and was probably linked to death and fertility.

The State God Tláloc was represented on a domestic level in figurines with 'goggles' and elaborate headdresses. However, at Oztoyahualco we also had evidence of patron gods related to particular families. A stucco rabbit sculpture was found on a basalt shrine, shaped like a Teotihuacan miniature temple, in one of the ritual patios.

Around the domestic ritual courtyards – of which there was one for each nuclear family – some activity areas related to ritual preparation were detected. There were also numerous funerary and offering pits.

Religion can be seen as a sphere of sociopolitical integration organized into a hierarchy in which the patron gods of family groups, barrio and occupational deities, the gods of specific priestly groups and, finally, state deities such as Tláloc were superimposed. Teotihuacan society was integrated mainly through religion, and the conception of the four directions of sacred space also permeated the city's domestic domain (Manzanilla 1993). Spatial patterning seems to have been established for the disposition of functional sectors which extended beyond the framework of nuclear families. We wish to emphasize that the affinity for order so patently manifest in the grid system of the city was also apparent in the domestic spheres.

The three-temple complexes found throughout the city may have been the centres of barrio groups – loci in which cult and exchange activities would take place for a number of specialized corporate groups living in apartment compounds around them.

A manufacturing centre

The manufactured goods of Teotihuacan had prestige all over Mesoamerica during the Classic Period. In particular high-quality pottery and prismatic blades of green obsidian were exchanged between élites. Other products, such as those derived from cactus and agave, as well as ritual paraphernalia, may have been exchanged with foreign groups (Millon 1993: 28). In the city, distinct manufacturing wards have been identified, specifically those for obsidian blade production around the Pyramid of the Moon, and ceramic production in the southeastern part of the city. Obsidian manufacture was specialized to the level of the type of artefact produced. Also identified were lapidary, shell, textile and feather-working

workshops and, around the Ciudadela, workshops making censer plaques, suggesting that the degree of craft specialization was correlated with the different circulation spheres.

Paulinyi (1981) suggests the existence of district groups which may have had a part in co-rulership: one is located to the west of the Great Compound; the second in the northwestern part of the valley; the third to the east of the Street of the Dead; the fourth on the eastern fringe of the city; and the fifth to the south of the San Lorenzo river.

The Merchants' Barrio and the Oaxaca Barrio were two foreign wards, but perhaps not the only ones. Recently, west Mexico pottery and figurines have been located in the western part of the city (Rubén Cabrera, personal communication, 1992). The Merchants' Barrio was probably inhabited by merchants from the Gulf Coast who lived in round houses and brought Maya pottery and Gulf Coast products. The Oaxaca Barrio may have been involved in the distribution of shell ornaments (Rattray 1987).

A redistributive centre

In our reconstruction of the economic organization of the Teotihuacan priesthood (Manzanilla 1992), we propose that the priests who administered Teotihuacan created different redistributive circuits to assure the maintenance of the bureaucracy as well as full-time state craftsmen. These redistributive networks ran parallel to other types of exchange systems: barter between producers, long-distance élite exchange, direct provisioning of sumptuary goods in colonies, foreign merchants using the city's distributive system and so on.

Teotihuacan was also the central place for a wide distribution of goods following definite commercial routes. One of these, perhaps the best defined, has been located in the Puebla-Tlaxcala region, where eighty Teotihuacan settlements are arranged in a corridor linking the capital to Cholula and then to the Oriental Basin and the Gulf Coast (García Cook 1981).

Sumptuary goods included feathers, jadeite and other greenstone minerals, cacao beans, incense (copal), rubber (Millon 1993), Atlantic and Pacific shells, avocados, cotton, perhaps also honey, animals from the tropical forest, Amate paper and other products.

A political capital

Nobody can deny that Teotihuacan was the capital of an incomparable state that established colonies in remote provinces of Mesoamerica. Yet, there are discrepancies with respect to its type of government. Some authors believe that Teoti-huacan was headed by a single lord or possibly two (Cabrera, Cowgill and Sugiyama 1990); others propose a priestly collective government (Manzanilla 1992).

Paulinyi (1981) suggests that Teotihuacan and Tula (a few centuries later) inaugurated a type of government characterized by the co-regency of three to seven lords. López Austin (1989) proposes that Teotihuacan was the first place where the transformation from lineage to state took place, a process in which the old lineage heads separated from the common people to form an autonomous group of bureaucrats, redistributers and nobles. The birth of the state would then have derived from the presence of groups of diverse origin and from the use of power to control a territory.

Millon (1993: 31) states that there is evidence of two military wards at Teotihuacan: one centred in Atetelco, in the southwestern part of the city, and the other – Techinantitla – in the northeastern section.

With the collapse of Teotihuacan a reordering of power spheres can be observed as can, during the Epiclassic, a process of 'balkanization' – the establishment of regional political units. Cholula, Cacaxtla, Xochicalco and Tula in the central highlands, El Tajín on the Gulf Coast, and various centres in the Mixtec mountains rose to power during the centuries after the decline of Teotihuacan.

A sacred capital

Teotihuacan was planned to be harmonious with the natural scenery. The main pyramids echoed the profiles of the principal mountains to the north, south and west. The processional avenue re-emphasized the importance of the Pyramid of the Moon with respect to the sacred mountain, the Cerro Gordo.

The division of the city into four sectors (the horizontal or 'earthly' dimension), together with the presence of an Underworld, a terrestrial and a celestial domain in the vertical one, as well as the astronomical orientation aligned on the heliacal setting of the Pleiades in the summer solstice, suggest that Teotihuacan was planned as a reproduction of the cosmos.

Since 1987, we have undertaken a geophysical, geological, palaeobiological and archaeological programme to study a system of tunnels under the ancient prehispanic city. This system was originally excavated by the Teotihuacanos themselves to extract porous volcanic materials for the construction of the city. Afterwards, the system seems to have been ritually used, evoking perhaps the concept of an Underworld and, particularly, the Tlalocan, the god Tláloc's Underworld.

Caves had multiple functions and meanings for prehispanic peoples: they were shelters, living sites, ritual places associated with lineage and passage rites, solar observatories, quarries, dwellings of the Gods of Water and those of Death, the mouth or womb of the Earth, the Underworld, a fantastic space and so on. Creation myths relate caves to sun, moon, foodstuffs and the emergence of human groups (Taube 1986). Caves were entrances to the Underworld (and therefore funerary chambers), but also were an access to the womb of the Earth (and thus a place where fertility rites took place). Water petition ceremonies for good harvests took place in caves, where water spirits dwelled (Weitlaner and Leonard 1959).

The Nahua-speaking peoples of Mexico associated three concepts with the Underworld: Mictlan, Tlillan and Tlalocan. According to

Anderson (1988: 153–4), Tlalocan was depicted as a place of great wealth, where there was no suffering and where maize was abundant, as were squash, amaranth, chile and flowers. In the Prayer to Tláloc in the Florentine Codex, translated by Sullivan (1965: 45), it is said that sustenance has not disappeared, but rather that the gods have hidden it in Tlalocan. In several examples of Náhuatl poetry, Tlalocan is portrayed as a place of beauty, where birds with lovely feathers sing on top of pyramids made of jade. It was also described as a construction consisting of four rooms around a patio, with four containers filled with water: one room was good, but the other three were associated with frosts, sterility and drought. It was further thought of as an underground space filled with water that connected the mountains with the sea. It was also a place where rivers originated.

The existence of caves in Teotihuacan is well known. Heyden (1981) reproduces the glyph of Teotihuacan from the Xólotl Codex which represents the two large pyramids overlying a cave with a person inside. It is likely that this figure refers to the oracles that were frequently located within caves, as indicated in the *Relación de Teotihuacan* (Soruco 1985: 107; 1991). In addition, toponyms such as Oztoyahualco and Oztotícpac also make reference to caves.

The general objective of our project was the location and definition of tunnels and caves which were of interest to archaeology because of their potential ritual or economic uses. The particular goals were to detect continuity of the tunnels throughout the northern part of the city, where the holes were not visible, and to locate primary contexts that would allow us to assess the following functions:

- the original extractive activities related to porous pyroclastic volcanic materials
- large-scale storage
- burials
- offerings related to fertility rites.

We thoroughly excavated four tunnels to the east of the Pyramid of the Sun. The third tunnel –

'Cueva de las Varillas' – is 50 metres long and had a vast entrance chamber, 18 metres in diameter, with seven small niches and a tunnel that crossed three small chambers. At one side it was connected to another chamber that had well-preserved funerary and storage contexts.

There were some hints of a cult that involved marine elements, such as different types of mother-of-pearl shells, a sting ray spine and fragments of marine turtle shells. We also found examples of foreign pottery from the Gulf Coast and the Mayan area.

The funerary chamber also contained modern and Aztec domestic material. Underneath the Aztec floors (fourteenth and fifteenth centuries) there were funerary and storage contexts of the Mazapa period (c. AD 930). Twelve Mazapa burials were found: a group of three seated adult burials facing south were excavated around a pillar left in the chamber; and two infant burials were placed near the adult ones at the level of their heads. All of these burials had mainly complete and ritually killed pottery vessels as offerings, as well as some projectile points. This first group appeared to be placed in the northeastern fringe of the chamber.

In the central sector of the chamber, and at a somewhat higher topographical level, there were seven new-born babies, some of them in a seated position and some in the foetal position; they were placed in an east–west band in the central part of the chamber. These burials had only triangles or rectangles of cut mica as offerings. There were also some hearths with Teotihuacan candeleros and projectile points. In the same chamber we found seven circular storage bin bases distributed in different sectors and at different depths within the stratum corresponding to the adult burials. We had already found six of these bases 50 metres inside the tunnel in an inner chamber, which had no apparent association with burials (Manzanilla 1994a, 1994b).

This chamber gave us evidence to confirm three of the functions of the caves predicted by the

5 *The 'Cueva del Pirul' tunnel located to the east of the Pyramid of the Sun, excavated in 1994 and 1995 (Manzanilla 1994).* (Photo: Linda Manzanilla)

6 *Burial 24 in foetal position near a new-born baby inside a jar base, in the 'Cueva del Pirul' tunnel.* (Photo: Linda Manzanilla)

7 *Two child burials (Burials 20 and 21) in the 'Cueva del Pirul' tunnel.* (Photo: Linda Manzanilla)

project: storage areas associated with fertility rituals in the womb of the Earth; burials as part of the Underworld concept; and baby burials as part of the Tlalocan idea.

The fourth tunnel ('Cueva del Pirul', fig. 5) provided similar data. In different chambers of the tunnel, near the entrance, we found fourteen burials: two seated adults (one with bilobulated skull), two young adults in foetal positions (fig. 6), four child burials and six perinatal burials. A set of six burials, mainly infants, was placed around a 'killed' hemispherical monochrome bowl with plastic design of the type known as 'Jiménez Sealed Brown' (Cobean 1990: 194–8). Cobean has related this type of bowl to the Coyotlatelco Sphere and to the Corral Complex; he suggests that they were used for drinking chocolate. In our excavations we have found numerous examples with different kinds of stamped motifs. Another type frequently found in contact with the disintegrated tuff consists of Negative painted bowls (Good and Obermeyer 1986: Plate 11).

Near two of the children (fig. 7) and one newborn baby, three complete and articulated dog skeletons (col. pl. 3) were found: two adults and a puppy, one of them with skeletal malformations. They could have been thought of as guides to the Underworld. Modest storage bin bases were also found in the first chamber of this tunnel. In another sector, a new-born baby was found inside a bowl near one of the seated adults, and an eight-month-old baby in a foetal position was covered with another bowl.

We can summarize our preliminary remarks for Teotihuacan in the following terms:

1. The system of tunnels and caves in the Teotihuacan Valley was originally a group of quarries, dating to the Patlachique or Tzacualli periods, for the extraction of porous volcanic materials. They are thus man-made. We must therefore rectify our previous idea, derived from Heyden (1975) and Millon (1973), that they were natural, because there is no natural phenomenon in volcanic contexts that can produce large or long holes except solid lava tubes, and this is not the case.

    There are radiocarbon dates from our caves (Beta 69912), as well as from the lower tunnel of the Pyramid of the Sun (M-1283; Millon, Drewitt, and Bennyhoff 1965: 33) and the Temple of the Feathered Serpent (col. pl. 4; Cabrera in Rattray 1991: 12), that are concentrated around the year AD 80. This could be evidence of great construction enterprises involving the tunnels and the main pyramids.

    Barba (1995) and I (Manzanilla 1994a) have speculated that, when the city was built, the sense of sacredness may be derived first from the fact that the construction material came from the subterranean world (in particular, the pyroclasts chosen were the small red ones, as if a sacred body were being built) and second from the use of the symbolically significant fire and water for making stucco, which thus formed part of the consecration act.

2. In the original settlement in the valley – consisting of three-temple plazas surrounded conspicuously by dwelling sites rather than the very dense urban site which Millon (1973) originally proposed – the quarry mouths were found very near these pyramid complexes, due to the fact that much construction material was needed for the raising of the pyramids themselves. When the plazas of these complexes were built, they seemed to be deliberately positioned on top of the tunnels. Whether or not there is a physical communi-cation between these tunnels and the plazas we do not yet know.

    Returning to the three-temple plazas arranged on top of the system of tunnels, we would propose that these open spaces were probably used for ball games with portable markers, as depicted in the Tlalocan mural at Tepantitla. It is a well-known fact that Teotihuacan did not have double-'I' or 'T' constructions used specifically as ball courts, so there is a possibility that the three-temple plazas, as well as the Street of the Dead and the huge plain behind the Pyramid of the Sun, could have been used for ball games and for diverse economic transactions. If this is true, the parallels with the Maya concept of the ball court as a portal of the Underworld would be evident. In fact, all the northern half of the city would have had tens of entrances to the Underworld.

3. Different rites could have been practised inside the tunnels. Brady and Stone (1986: 19) proposed that the Naj Tunich cave in Guatemala could have been a burial place for members of Maya royalty. There is a great probability that this is also true for many caves ritually used during the Classic Period in central Mexico.

    The hypothesis is that the important bureaucrats of the ancient city of Teotihuacan were buried in this Underworld. Many of the polished stone funerary masks that come mainly from private collections, but also from prehispanic looting, may have come from these burials. In fact, we have evidence that the people who used Coyotlatelco, Mazapa and Aztec ceramics dwelled in these caves and looted them. Fragments of human bones, fresco-painted ceramics, painted slate and other archaeological materials have come from a mixed fill of more than 4 metres that sealed many of the caves. As previously mentioned, this was material stacked inside the cave system either by the Coyotlatelco people around AD 680 or by the Teotihuacanos themselves.

In this cave system the Epiclassic–Early Postclassic people constructed a shrine for the *tlaloques* (the assistants of Tláloc), represented by the seven babies deposited in the central part of the funerary chamber of the Varillas Tunnel, precisely underneath a hole in the cavity's roof, a hole that may have allowed the pouring of rain water on top of the shrine. The adult burials were seated with their backs to a pillar left to prevent the collapsing of the cavity, and facing south, as if they were guardians of the Underworld.

Other types of rites practised inside the tunnels could have been related to fertility ceremonies in the womb of the Earth. In fact, Armillas (Navarrete, personal communication) mentioned the fact that tons of storage vessel fragments were found when the La Gruta Restaurant was enlarged. Large-scale ritualized storage is one of the main aspects we are interested in.

In the Cueva de las Varillas we found thirteen bases of storage bins, seven of them surrounding the burial area and six in an inner chamber 50 metres from the entrance and too far to be practical for economic use. We believe these formed part of fertility propitiation rites.

4. The Pyramid of the Sun at Teotihuacan is the only structure not constructed of the porous volcanic material, *tezontle*, derived from the tunnels. Instead it was built mainly with earth and small fragments of tuff (5 to 10 centimetres; Rattray 1974) that generally overlie the pyroclasts.

In 1989, we interviewed old men and women about the caves at Teotihuacan. Different people mentioned the myth that in olden days, in February, a man was seen coming from under the Pyramid of the Sun carrying maize, amaranth, green beans, and courgettes. Many also added that under the Pyramid of the Sun

there were *chinampa*-like ditched fields where all these foodstuffs were harvested.

The concept of a mountain of sustenance – the Tonacatépetl of the Nahua tradition – is frequent in Mesoamerica, as is the sacred mountain with a cave from which water emerged (Freidel, Schele and Parker 1993: 430). We propose that the Pyramid of the Sun was conceived of as a Tonacatépetl or 'mountain of sustenance'; this idea is reinforced by the mention made in the *Relación de Teotihuacan* (Paso y Troncoso 1979: 222) in which the idol on the summit of the pyramid was Tonacateuctli. This monumental construction is the only one built with organic soil coming from the alluvial plain, perhaps from the Acolman area. Other 'mountains of sustenance' were built in rain-producing mountains such as Tetzcotzingo and Mount Tláloc, as Townsend states (1993: 38). Finally, the Templo Mayor (Great Temple) of Tenochtitlan would be a continuation of this tradition (Broda 1987).

This pyramid might have synthesized three concepts intimately related: the Tonacatépetl, the main temple for the State God Tláloc, and the sacred mountain, the centre of the universe, represented as the centre of the four-petal flower, as López Austin (1989) suggested.

5. Teotihuacan was built as a sacred copy of the cosmos. Its terrestrial plane is divided into the four quarters of the universe; it has a celestial plane, the sky itself and the summits of the temples, but also an Underworld represented by the system of tunnels under the northern half of the city.

Its main avenue connected the natural sacred mountain of Cerro Gordo, where Tobriner (1972) detected a cave of special significance, with the Pyramid of the Sun (the artificial 'mountain of sustenance') and the spring area to the south (Townsend 1993: 41). As Townsend states, following Aveni and Broda, the East–West Avenue traces the path of the Pleiades in the summer solstice.

6. In a recent study of Nahuat-speaking groups in the Sierra de Puebla region of Mexico, Knab (1991) describes a myth that mentions the geography of the Underworld or Tlalocan, as conceived by the inhabitants of San Miguel Tzinacapan. In the myth, the caves are considered to be entrances to the Underworld:

- The northern entrance, Mictalli or Miquitalan, is represented by a 'cave of the winds' and is the access to the world of the dead. Tobriner (1972) made reference to a gorge on the northeastern slope of Cerro Gordo at the northern fringe of the Teotihuacan Valley, with a cave that emitted a sound of water. A map dating to 1580 represents this gorge on the southeastern portion of the hill. Tobriner (1972: 113) also suggested that the Street of the Dead in Teotihuacan was built pointing towards Cerro Gordo because of the association of this mountain with the God of Water.
- The southern entrance is called Atotonican and is a place of warmth, a hot spring that produces vapour and clouds in the back of a cave. It is well known that the area of springs is situated in the southwestern sector of the valley, another parallel with the myth.
- The eastern access is called Apan, a large lake in the Underworld that joins the sea. The lacustrine basin of Apan is located precisely to the east of the Teotihuacan Valley.
- The western entrance is a mountain called Tonalan, where the sun stops on its voyage. Mount Tonalan is actually a low mountain located on the northwestern boundary of the valley, between Cerro Gordo and Cerro Malinalco.

It is probable that the myth of the Nahuat speakers in the Sierra de Puebla is derived from a version based on the sacred geography of the Teotihuacan Valley, but it is equally probable that both have their source in an archetypical Mesoamerican conception of the Underworld. Thus, the construction of sacred space is a tradition derived from Formative times and culminates with the building of cities as models of the cosmos.

As mentioned earlier, Teotihuacan could have also been the place where sacred time was created, as was recently proposed for the Temple of Quetzalcóatl (López Austin, López Luján, and Sugiyama 1991). Millon (1993: 23) also suggests that the tunnel under the Pyramid of the Sun '…came to be seen as the focus of a creation myth in which it was portrayed as the place where the present era began, where humankind came into being, and where the present cycle of time was born'. Teotihuacan society was integrated mainly through religion, and the conception of the four directions of sacred space permeated both the planning of the city as a whole and its domestic domain (Manzanilla 1993). Religion was represented in three levels: state religion, district or barrio gods, and lineage deities.

Teotihuacan was thus the archetype of the Mesoamerican civilized city, the most sacred realm, and the mythic Tollan where crafts flourished. It inaugurated a new era in the settlement pattern of the region, an era that has not yet ended.

A diachronic view

We consider that there were two epochs in the history of Teotihuacan. The first belongs to the Patlachique–Tzacualli phases, with settlement concentrated in the so-called 'Old City', the northwestern sector of the valley. This sector is characterized by a vast tongue of pyroclastic materials where different caves and tunnels were excavated by the Teotihuacanos to extract the porous volcanic materials for their constructions.

Three-temple plazas were the main architectural groups of this settlement and may be also the congregational centres of ward groups. The

Pyramids of the Sun and the Moon also belong to three-temple plazas. These groups could be related to the system of tunnels and caves that we propose crosses the northern part of the city (Manzanilla *et al.* 1989; Manzanilla 1994a, 1994b).

The settlement density of this epoch was light and not continuous. The San Juan alluvial plain was devoted to cultivation and all the constructions were placed in the northern half of the valley.

Millon (1993: 25) believes that this first epoch was an era of strong rulers who demonstrated their power by building huge constructions such as the main pyramids, the Ciudadela, and the Street of the Dead. As Millon states (1993: 24), 'ideology would have played a critical integrative role, supporting the state in maintaining order in a city now swollen with thousands of ethnically diverse newcomers...'

The Pyramid of the Moon, probably dedicated to the Great Goddess, would have been the culmination of the avenue and would have been framed by the sacred mountain, the Cerro Gordo (Millon 1993: 24). The Pyramid of the Sun, according to Millon, would have been devoted to the Great Goddess and to the Storm God. My guess is that it was devoted to Tonacatecuhtli (God of Sustenance), an advocation of Tláloc.

The construction of the Temple of the Feathered Serpent would have been, in Millon's view (1993: 25), an enterprise related to 'an ambitious new ruler with a passion for immortality...', and would have been related to the planet Venus and a cult of sacred war and sacrifice, that has been called the 'star war'.

During the second epoch, beginning in AD 250, the city acquired an orthogonal configuration. From the Tlamimilolpa phase onwards, elements of urban planning are clear in the new city. The multifamily apartment compounds represent the new domestic architectural unit.

Millon (1993: 26–7) has proposed that there was a period of reaction and political reform which transformed rulership into collective leadership, and intensified religiosity. Expansion continued into other parts of Mesoamerica.

The city grew and invaded the alluvial plain. Excessive rural–urban migration, deforestation of nearby mountains to obtain wood for construction and fuel for domestic use and lime-burning, soil erosion, over-exploitation of aquifers, problems with food production, inadequacy of the system to harmonize ethnic and social groups of diverse interests were the characteristic of this second epoch.

The core of the city was finally burned and looted. Incursions of nomadic groups, agricultural collapse, powerful marginal groups and the blocking of supply routes have all been cited as factors involved in the city's collapse. Millon (1988) also mentions that the causes of Teotihuacan's end were bad administration, inflexibility with respect to change, the existence of an inefficient bureaucracy, and the deterioration of exchange routes.

Acknowledgements

I thank the following people for their participation in the domestic archaeology project: Luis Barba and Agustín Ortiz for the geophysical and geochemical exploration, as well as for the chemical studies; Raúl Valadez for the palaeofaunal analysis; Neusa Hidalgo, Javier González, and Emily McClung for the palaeobotanical data; Beatriz Ludlow and Emilio Ibarra for the pollen information; Judith Zurita for the phytolith analysis; Magalí Civera and Mario Millones for the osteological analyses; Cynthia Hernández for the lithic analyses; Miguel Angel Jiménez for the ceramic distribution maps; Edith Ortiz for the domestic ideology research; and the Graphic Department of the Institute of Anthropological Research of the National Autonomous University of Mexico for their invaluable help. This interdisciplinary research on domestic life was funded by the Institute of Anthropological Research of the National Autonomous University of Mexico (UNAM).

With respect to the study of tunnels and caves, I thank the following people for their participation in particular studies: AnnCorinne Freter from Ohio University for the obsidian hydration dates; Luis Barba and Agustín Ortiz for the geophysical and geochemical prospection; Claudia Trejo for the chemical studies; Raúl Valadez for the palaeofaunal analysis; Emily McClung de Tapia, Diana Martínez, Rebeca Rodríguez, and Cristina Adriano for the palaeobotanical data; Emilio Ibarra, Ruth Castañeda and Oanna del Castillo for the pollen information; Judith Zurita and Gabriela Silva for the phytolith analysis; Cynthia Hernández and Marcela Zapata for the lithic analyses; Miguel Angel Jiménez and Claudia López for the ceramic distribution maps; Claudia López for the ceramic study; Rocío Arrellín for the osteological analysis; T. Douglas Price and William H. Middleton of the University of Wisconsin-Madison for the strontium isotope study; Edith Ortiz for the haemoglobin study; Rocío Vargas for the fossil DNA study; Edith Ortiz, Cynthia Hernández, Miguel Angel Jiménez, Mauricio Garduño, Rocío Arrellín, Claudia López, Marcela Zapata, Beatriz Maldonado, Rossana Enríquez, and Alfredo Feria for assistance in the exploration of the tunnels, and the Graphic Department of the Institute of Anthropological Research of the National Autonomous University of Mexico for their invaluable help.

This research was funded by the Institute of Anthropological Research and by Grant DGAPA-UNAM IN214694 of the National Autonomous University of Mexico (UNAM); by Grants n.P218CC00892832, H9106-0060, and 400358-5-5412-S of the National Council of Science and Technology of Mexico (CONACYT), and by Grant FAMSI n.95007 of the Foundation for the Advancement of Mesoamerican Studies, Inc., and it was undertaken with permission of the Archaeological Council of the National Institute of Anthropology and History (INAH). The geophysical work was also partially supported by an internal grant IGF-02-9102.

I would also like to thank doctors Zoltán de Cserna and Gerardo Sánchez Rubio of the Institute of Geology; José Lugo Hubp of the Institute of Geography; Jaime Urrutia and Dante Morán of the Institute of Geophysics, National Autonomous University of Mexico, for their advice and suggestions at different stages of the geological research at Teotihuacan. We also thank the students of the Engineering Faculty of the University and those of the National School of Anthropology and History for their participation. The radiocarbon dates were obtained from Beta Analytic, Inc.

References

Anderson, Arthur J.O. (1988) 'A look into Tlalocan', *Smoke and Mist. Mesoamerican Studies in Memory of Thelma D. Sullivan*, J.K. Josserand and K. Dakin (eds), BAR International Series 402, 151–9.

Aveni, Anthony F., Horst Hartung and Beth Buckingham (1978) 'The pecked cross symbol in ancient Mesoamerica', *Science* 202, 267–79.

Barba, Luis, Beatriz Ludlow, Linda Manzanilla and Raúl Valadez (1987) 'La vida doméstica en Teotihuacan. Un estudio interdisciplinario', *Ciencia y desarrollo* 77, XIII, Nov./Dec., 21–3.

Brady, James E. and Andrea Stone (1986) 'Naj Tunich: Entrance to the Maya Underworld', *Archaeology* 39, 6, Nov./Dec., 18–25.

Brady, James E. and George Veni (1992) 'Man-made and pseudo-Karst caves: the implication of subsurface features within Maya centres', *Geoarchaeology: An International Journal* 7 (2), 149–67.

Broda, J. (1987) 'Templo Mayor as ritual space', *The Great Temple of Tenochtitlan. Center and Periphery in the Aztec World*, J. Broda, D. Carrasco and E. Matos Moctezuma (eds), 61–123. Berkeley: University of California Press.

Cabrera, Rubén, George L. Cowgill and Saburo Sugiyama (1990) 'El Proyecto Templo de

Quetzalcóatl y la práctica a gran escala del sacrificio humano', *La Epoca Clásica: Nuevos Hallazgos, Nuevas Ideas*, A. Cardós de Méndez (coordinator), 123–46. México: INAH.

Cobean, Robert H. (1990) *La cerámica de Tula, Hidalgo* (Colección Científica 215). México: INAH.

Durán, Fray D. (1967) *Historia de las Indias de Nueva España e Islas de la Tierra Firme* Vol. I. México: Editorial Porrúa.

Freidel, David A. (1981) 'The political economics of residential dispersion among the Lowland Maya', *Lowland Maya Settlement Patterns*, W. Ashmore (ed.), 371–82. Albuquerque: University of New Mexico.

Freidel, David, Linda Schele and Joy Parker (1993) *Maya Cosmos. Three Thousand Years on the Shaman's Path*. New York: William Morrow and Co., Inc.

García Cook, Angel (1981) 'The historical importance of Tlaxcala in the cultural development of the central highlands', *Supplement to the Handbook of Middle American Indians, Archaeology*, I, J.A. Sabloff (ed.), 244–76. Austin: University of Texas Press.

Good, Kenneth and Gerald Obermeyer (1986) 'Excavations at Oxtotipac (TT82)', *The Toltec Period Occupation of the Valley. Part 1. Excavations and Ceramics, The Teotihuacan Valley Project Final Report, 4* (Occasional Papers in Anthropology 13), W.T. Sanders (ed.), 195–265. Pennsylvania: The Pennsylvania State University.

Heyden, D. (1975) 'An interpretation of the cave underneath the Pyramid of the Sun in Teotihuacan, Mexico', *American Antiquity* 40, 2, 131–47.

Heyden, D. (1981) 'Caves, gods and myths: world views and planning in Teotihuacan', *Mesoamerican Sites and World Views*, E.P. Benson (ed.), 1–39. Washington DC: Dumbarton Oaks.

Knab, Tim J. (1991) 'Geografía del inframundo', *Estudios de Cultura Náhuatl* 21, 31–57.

Krickeberg, Walter (1949) *Felsplastik und Felsbilder bei den Kulturvolkern Altamerikas mit besonderer Berücksichtigung Mexicos*, 206–18. Berlin: Palmen-Verlag.

Linné, Sigvald (1942) *Mexican Highland Cultures. Archaeological Researches at Teotihuacan, Calpulalpan and Chalchicomula in 1934–35*. Stockholm: The Ethnographical Museum of Sweden.

López Austin, Alfredo (1989) 'La historia de Teotihuacan', *Teotihuacan*, 13–35. México: El Equilibrista, Citicorp/Citibank.

López Austin, Alfredo, Leonardo López Luján and Saburo Sugiyama (1991) 'The Temple of Quetzalcóatl at Teotihuacan. Its possible ideological significance', *Ancient Mesoamerica* 2, 93–105.

Manzanilla, Linda (1985) 'El sitio de Cuanalan en el marco de las comunidades pre-urbanas del Valle de Teotihuacan', *Mesoamérica y el Centro de México*, J. Monjarás-Ruiz, E. Pérez Rocha and R. Brambila (ed.), 133–78. México: INAH.

Manzanilla, Linda (1988–9) 'The study of room function in a residential compound at Teotihuacan, Mexico', *Origini, Giornate in onore di Salvatore Maria Puglisi* XIV, 175–86. Rome: Universitá la Sapienza.

Manzanilla, Linda (1992) 'The economic organization of the Teotihuacan priesthood: hypotheses and considerations', *Art, Ideology and the City of Teotihuacan*, J.C. Berlo (ed.), 321–38. Washington DC: Dumbarton Oaks.

Manzanilla, Linda (ed.) (1993) *Anatomía de un conjunto residencial teotihuacano en Oztoyahualco*, 2 vols. México: UNAM, Instituto de Investigaciones Antropológicas.

Manzanilla, Linda (1994a) 'Geografía sagrada e inframundo en Teotihuacan', *Antropológicas* 11, 53–65.

Manzanilla, Linda (1994b) 'Las cuevas en el mundo mesoamericano', *Ciencias* 36, 59–66.

Manzanilla, Linda and Luis Barba (1990) 'The study of activities in Classic households. Two case studies from Cobá and Teotihuacan', *Ancient Mesoamerica* I, 1, 41–9.

Manzanilla, Linda and Emilie Carreón (1991) 'A Teotihuacan censer in a residential context. An interpretation', *Ancient Mesoamerica* 2, 2, 299–307.

Manzanilla, Linda and Leonardo López Luján (eds) (1994) *Historia antigua de México*. México: INAH–UNAM–Porrúa.

Manzanilla, Linda, L. Barba, R. Chávez, J. Arzate and L. Flores (1989) 'El inframundo de Teotihuacan. Geofísica y Arqueología', *Ciencia y desarrollo* xv, 85, 21–35.

Manzanilla, Linda, L. Barba, R. Chávez, A. Tejero, G. Cifuentes and N. Peralta (1994) 'Caves and geophysics: An approximation to the underworld of Teotihuacan, Mexico', *Archaeometry* 36, 1, 141–57.

Marcus, Joyce (1983) 'On the nature of the Mesoamerican city', *Prehistoric Settlement Patterns*.

Essays in Honor of Gordon R. Willey, E.Z. Vogt and R.M. Leventhal (eds), 195–242. Cambridge: University of New Mexico Press and Peabody Museum of Archaeology and Ethnology.

McClung de Tapia, Emily (1979) 'Plants and Subsistence in the Teotihuacan Valley AD 100–750'. Ph.D. Dissertation. Ann Arbor: University Microfilms.

McClung de Tapia, Emily (1980) 'Interpretación de restos botánicos procedentes de sitios arqueológicos', *Anales de Antropología* XVII, 149–65.

Millon, René (1968) 'Urbanization at Teotihuacan: The Teotihuacan mapping project', *Actas y Memorias del XXXVII Congreso Internacional de Americanistas*, Argentina 1966, 105–20. Buenos Aires: Depto. de Publicaciones Científicas Argentinas.

Millon, René (1973) *Urbanization at Teotihuacan. The Teotihuacan Map. Part One: Text*. Austin: University of Texas Press.

Millon, René (1988) 'The last years of Teotihuacan dominance', *The Collapse of Ancient States and Civilizations*, N. Yoffee and G.L. Cowgill (eds), 102–64. Tucson: The University of Arizona Press.

Millon, René (1993) 'The place where time began. An archaeologist's interpretation of what happened in Teotihuacan history', *Teotihuacan. Art from the City of the Gods*, K. Berrin and E. Pasztory (eds), 16–43. San Francisco: Thames and Hudson, The Fine Arts Museums of San Francisco.

Millon, René, Bruce Drewitt and James A. Bennyhoff (1965) *The Pyramid of the Sun at Teotihuacán: 1959 Investigations*. (Transactions n.s., v. 55, part 6, September.) Philadelphia: The American Philosophical Society.

Monzón, Martha (1989) *Casas prehispánicas en Teotihuacan*. México, Toluca: Instituto Mexiquense de Cultura.

Paso y Troncoso, Francisco del (1979) *Papeles de Nueva España. Segunda Serie: Geografía y Estadística, Relaciones Geográficas de la Diócesis de México*. México: Editorial Cosmos.

Paulinyi, Z. (1981) 'Capitals in Pre-Aztec Central Mexico', *Acta Orientalia Academiae Scientiarum Hungaricae* XXXV, 2–3, 315–50.

Rattray, Evelyn Childs (1974) 'Some clarifications on the Early Teotihuacan Ceramic Sequence', XLI *Congreso Internacional de Americanistas, México D.F.*, 364–8.

Rattray, Evelyn Childs (1987) 'Los barrios foráneos de Teotihuacan', *Teotihuacan. Nuevos datos, nuevas síntesis y nuevos problemas*, E. McClung de Tapia and E. Childs Rattray (eds), 243–73. México: UNAM, IIA.

Rattray, Evelyn Childs (1991) 'Fechamientos por radiocarbono en Teotihuacan', *Arqueología* 6, 3–18.

Sánchez Alaniz, José Ignacio (1989), 'Las unidades habitacionales en Teotihuacan: el caso de Bidasoa'. Tesis de licenciatura en Arqueología. México: ENAH.

Sanders, William T., Jeffrey R. Parsons and Robert S. Santley (1979) *The Basin of Mexico. Ecological Processes in the Evolution of a Civilization*. New York: Academic Press.

Séjourné, L. (1966) *Arquitectura y pintura en Teotihuacan*. México: Siglo XXI.

Soruco Saenz, Enrique (1985) 'Una cueva ceremonial en Teotihuacan'. Tesis de licenciatura en Arqueología. México: ENAH.

Soruco Saenz, Enrique (1991) 'Una cueva ceremonial en Teotihuacan y sus implicaciones astronómicas religiosas', *Arqueoastronomía y etnoastronomía en Mesoamérica*, J. Broda, S. Iwaniszewski, and L. Maupomé (eds), 291–6. México: UNAM.

Spence, Michael (1966) 'Los talleres de obsidiana de Teotihuacan', XI *Mesa Redonda: El Valle de Teotihuacan y su entorno*, 213–18. México: Sociedad Mexicana de Antropología.

Starbuck, David (1975) 'Man-Animal Relationships in Pre-Columbian Central Mexico'. Ph.D. Dissertation. Yale University, Department of Anthropology.

Storey, Rebecca (1992) *Life and Death in the Ancient City of Teotihuacan. A Modern Paleodemographic Synthesis*. Tuscaloosa: The University of Alabama Press.

Storey, Rebecca and Randolph J. Widmer (1989) 'Household and community structure of a Teotihuacan apartment compound: S3W1:33 of the Tlajinga Barrio', *Households and Communities*, S. MacEachern, D.J.W. Archer and R.D. Garvin (eds), 407–15. Calgary: The Archaeological Association of the University of Calgary.

Sullivan, T.D. (1965) 'A prayer to Tláloc', *Estudios de Cultura Náhuatl* V, 39–55.

Taube, Karl A. (1986) 'The Teotihuacan cave of origin', *Res* 12, 51–82.

Tichy, Franz (1983) 'El patrón de asentamiento con sistema radial en la meseta central de México: sistemas ceque en Mesoamérica?', *Jahrbuch für Geschichte von Staat, Wirtschaft und Gesellschaft*

Lateinamerikas 20, 61–84. Köln/Wien: Böhlau Verlag.

Tobriner, Stephen (1972) 'The fertile mountain: An investigation of Cerro Gordo's importance to the town plan and iconography of Teotihuacan', *Teotihuacan* XI, 103–15. Mesa Redonda, México: Sociedad Mexicana de Antropología.

Townsend, Richard F. (1993) 'Paisaje y símbolo', *La antigua América. El arte de los parajes sagrados*, R.F. Townsend (ed.), 29–47. México: Grupo Azabache, The Art Institute of Chicago.

Uruñuela y Ladrón de Guevara, Gabriela y Patricia Plunket Nagoda (1995) *Proyecto Tetimpa. Informe técnico al Consejo de Arqueología. Primera temporada (noviembre 1993–julio 1994)*. Puebla,

México: Archivo Técnico del INAH, Universidad de las Américas.

Valadez Azúa, R. (1993) 'Macrofósiles faunísticos', *Anatomía de un conjunto residencial teotihuacano en Oztoyahualco*, L. Manzanilla (ed.), vol. 2., 729–825. México: UNAM.

Valadez, Raúl and Linda Manzanilla (1988) 'Restos faunísticos y áreas de actividad en una unidad habitacional de la antigua ciudad de Teotihuacan', *Revista Mexicana de Estudios Antropológicos*, XXXIV, 1, 147–68.

Weitlaner, Roberto and Juan Leonard (1959)'De la cueva al palacio', *Esplendor del México Antiguo*, Centro de Investigaciones Antropológicas de México, 933–56. México.

2. Water and Fire: Archaeology in the Capital of the Mexica Empire

Leonardo López Luján

The archaeology of Mexico-Tenochtitlan

As recently as two decades ago, systematized information on Mexico-Tenochtitlan, the metropolis of the most important Mesoamerican state at the time of the Europeans' arrival, was extremely scarce. Unlike other cities such as Tikal, Monte Albán and Teotihuacan, the capital of the Mexica (Aztec) empire was never the site of extensive excavation projects that were to bring its principal remains to light. The explanation for this archaeological ignorance is very simple. In 1521, the island occupied by the twin cities of Mexico-Tenochtitlan and Mexico-Tlatelolco fell into the hands of the Spanish conquerors (fig. 8). After the victory, Hernán Cortés took the historic decision to destroy the metropolis which had been home to between 200,000 and 300,000 inhabitants and covered an area of 13.5 square kilometres (Rojas 1992: 31–5, 57–84). On its ruins was founded Mexico City, the capital of New Spain and, from 1821 onwards, the capital of the Mexican Republic. Obviously, colonial and modern buildings caused problems for archaeologists. In fact, it was only in exceptional circumstances and in relatively limited areas that it had been possible to bring to light small portions of the prehispanic city.

Despite this serious constraint, those researching Mexica society have one clear advantage over colleagues studying the Maya area or sites like Monte Albán and Teotihuacan: numerous documentary sources from the sixteenth century. In some ways, it could be said that the abundance of historical records of life in Tenochtitlan made up for the lack of archaeological exploration on a large scale. For example, the graphic and written information on the Templo Mayor (Great Temple) of Tenochtitlan was enough to reveal the history of the most important religious building of the empire from its founding, through its multiple extensions and right up to the time when it was completely dismantled. In fact, no other monument in Ancient Mexico so commanded the attention of both natives and outsiders alike or was the subject of such lengthy descriptions as this double temple dedicated to Huitzilopochtli (the God of Sun and War) and Tláloc (the Rain God). All kinds of information relating to the Great Temple can be found in the indigenous pictographic documents and Náhuatl language texts; in the accounts of the European conquerors who saw it functioning and witnessed its destruction; in the narratives of the Spanish friars, which were often based on the native tradition; and even in the fantastical writings, illustrated with extravagant engravings, which circulated in Europe from the sixteenth century (León-Portilla 1987).

Little by little, the information contained in historical sources was augmented by the remains of the Mexica culture accidentally dug up during development work and the construction of buildings. But it was not until the end of the eighteenth century that spectacular finds such as the Stone of the Sun, the sculpture of Coatlicue and the Stone of Tízoc prompted scholars of prehispanic Mexico to compare archaeological data and historical data in a systematic way.

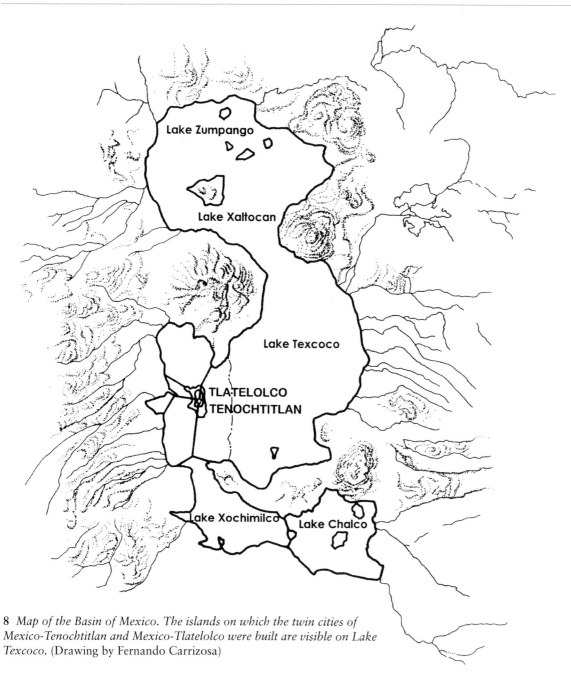

8 *Map of the Basin of Mexico. The islands on which the twin cities of Mexico-Tenochtitlan and Mexico-Tlatelolco were built are visible on Lake Texcoco.* (Drawing by Fernando Carrizosa)

Unfortunately, many of the accidental discoveries made during the nineteenth and twentieth centuries were destroyed or else fell easy prey to pillaging, thus swelling national and foreign collections. Others, fortunately, were recorded *in situ* and were rescued by archaeologists during salvage work, thus becoming part of the collections of the Mexico City National Museum of Anthropology (Boone 1987).

9 *Aerial photograph of the ruins of the Sacred Precinct of Mexico-Tlatelolco, excavated in the 1940s, 1970s and 1980s.* (Photo: courtesy of Aerofotoservicios S.A. de C.V.)

The Templo Mayor project (1978–97)

The first large-scale excavation on the ancient island of Mexico goes back to the 1940s (López Luján 1989). We owe this unique work to Pablo Martínez del Río and Antonieta Espejo, who explored the portico of the Church of Santiago and retrieved the remains of the Templo Mayor of Tlatelolco from the rubble. After twenty years of inactivity, work was continued in the same area. As a result of new fieldwork, a number of religious buildings were exposed, together with thousands of human burials, which also formed part of the Tlatelolco Sacred Precinct (fig. 9).

By contrast, the large-scale exploration in the Sacred Precinct of Tenochtitlan had to wait until February 1978, when the sculpture representing

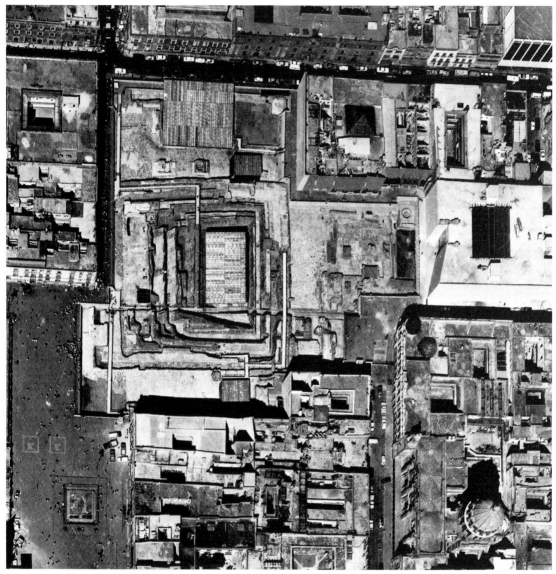

10 *Aerial photograph of the ruins of the Sacred Precinct of Mexico-Tenochtitlan, excavated between 1978 and 1997.* (Photo: courtesy of Aerofotoservicios S.A. de C.V.)

Coyolxauhqui, the Moon Goddess, was accidentally discovered. Given the enormous scientific importance of this monolith and the surrounding area, the National Institute of Anthropology and History (Instituto Nacional de Antropología e Historia – INAH) decided to organize a long-term research project entitled 'Proyecto Templo Mayor' (Great Temple Project). So far, five campaigns of fieldwork have been carried out. The first three (1978–82, 1987 and 1989) were coordinated by Eduardo Matos Moctezuma, and the last two (1991–2 and 1994–7) by the author of this paper. During this time we have been able to retrieve a considerable part of one of the most prominent ritual sites of the Mesoamerican world (fig. 10). Among the more significant discoveries are the ruins of the Templo Mayor of Tenochtitlan and 14 neighbouring buildings, 134 offerings, more than 9,000 artefacts and a considerable collection of sculptures and wall paintings. The area excavated extensively measures 1.3 hectares. Nonetheless, it must be noted that although this area might seem large, it is only equivalent to 0.1 per cent of the total area of the twin cities.

In 1983 the archaeological site was opened to visitors for the first time. That same year, once the first phase of excavation was completed, our project proceeded to the stage of laboratory analysis. As a result of that phase, more than 130 papers have been published by members of the project as well as guest researchers (Gutiérrez Solana 1989). Thanks to the enormous importance of the excavated area, information of the highest quality was made available which has enabled us to verify, complement and even reconsider many suppositions which we formerly held to be true (Matos Moctezuma 1988; Broda, Carrasco and Matos Moctezuma 1987; López Luján 1994). Finally, I would like to mention that in October 1987 what was without doubt one of our main objectives was realized: the opening of the Museum of the Templo Mayor. The premises presently house the project headquarters and eight rooms where archaeological material from the excavations is exhibited.

Recent work on the House of Eagles

The House of Eagles (also known as the Precinct of the Eagle Warriors) is one of the most impressive finds from the first phase of fieldwork. It consists of a large platform with an L-shaped ground plan, whose staircase is decorated with two sculptures in the shape of eagle heads (col. pl. 6). In 1981, after exploring the inside of this building, an older substructure was found which is contemporary with Stage IVb of the Templo Mayor (*c*. AD 1469). It is characterized by the presence of several inner rooms which are in a perfect state of conservation because they were buried ritually and with great care when it was decided that a new extension

would be built. We know that in prehispanic times one entered this substructure by two staircases which extended from the square to the wide portico which was supported by a colonnade. To reach the main room one had to pass through a door guarded by two ceramic sculptures which represent full-length individuals dressed in eagle costumes. From the main room, where the altar was situated, the visitor passed into the remaining rooms through a passageway protected by two huge skeletal figures, also made of fired clay. In this way, one arrived at a rectangular patio bordered by two rooms. Each room contained an altar and a pair of ceramic braziers decorated with the face of the Rain God.

Almost all the inside walls of the House of Eagles are decorated with beautiful paintings painted on clay and long polychrome benches. The latter are made up of two panels. The upper panel is a frieze depicting undulating snakes in bas-relief. The lower panel shows processions of armed warriors who merge in a *zacatapayolli*, a ball of grass to which the Mexicas (Aztecs) would stick the bloodstained agave thorns used during the ritual of self-sacrifice. The rich iconography of the benches tells us that the blood offering was one of the main ceremonies carried out in the building. What is more, the iconography is a magnificent example of the Mexica taste for imitating the artistic styles of more ancient civilizations, such as those of Teotihuacan and Tula, which flourished in the Basin of Mexico several centuries earlier (Fuente 1990; Matos Moctezuma and López Luján 1993). In this instance, we are looking at a 'revival' of the Burnt Palace, one of the many buildings excavated by the Mexicas at the Toltec capital of Tula, which by this time lay in ruins.

Thanks to the collaboration between the INAH, the Autonomous University of Mexico (Universidad Nacional Autónoma de México – UNAM) and the Mesoamerican Archive and Research Project of Princeton University, we have been able to continue our work on this exceptional building. During the last two phases of fieldwork

(1991–2 and 1994–7), a small team of archae-ologists, biologists, chemists and restorers undertook new studies which aim to shed light on the functions and activities which took place in the House of Eagles. Our first aim was to reconstruct the ritual activities which were carried out in this place on a daily basis. With the help of the team coordinated by Luis A. Barba, we cut out a tiny cylindrical piece from each square meter of the stucco floor, retrieving in this way more than five hundred samples. By means of microchemical analysis of these samples, we found deposits of carbonates, phosphates, fatty acids, albumin (the main protein in blood) and other compounds. Once it was transferred to the computer, this information helped us to deduce that specific activities took place in particular parts of the building: the offering of food to the gods, self-sacrifice and the burning of copal incense (Ortiz *et al.* 1996).

The next task was to detect and excavate all types of features buried beneath the stucco floors of the House of Eagles. For this purpose we used two magnetometers and a resistivity meter, instruments which helped us to discover magnetic and electric anomalies produced by several of the buried offerings, a drainage system and a smaller, older building. We continued to excavate in those places showing the greatest anomalies. After a year of meticulous work, we were able to record in detail and recover, among other things, eight offerings and a burial, which were found beneath floors, altars and staircases. The burial was that of an adult whose corpse was incinerated and remains crushed and reincinerated. Three ceramic urns were used as containers for the bones and a rich offering consisting of cotton textiles, blood-letting implements for self-sacrifice, copper needles, eagles' claws, feline teeth, obsidian sceptres and ornaments made of gold sheet. Of the three urns, the one that stands out is a Teotihuacan vessel which dates from the Classic period. Without a doubt, this urn was the fruit of excavation carried out by the fifteenth-century

Mexicas in the ruins of Teotihuacan, which had long been abandoned by that time.

Because the House of Eagles is presently partially buried beneath Justo Sierra Street, the decision was made to dig two long tunnels beneath the visitors' walkway in the archaeological zone (López Luján 1995). Many months of hard work exposed two new large-proportioned rooms decorated with wall paintings, and over thirty metres of benches with their polychromy almost completely intact. The most amazing find made inside the tunnels dates from September 1994: two huge ceramic sculptures were dug up which flanked a previously undiscovered entrance (López Luján and Mercado, 1996). Both are similar in proportion to the two sculptures of individuals dressed in eagle costumes which are currently on display in the Museum of the Templo Mayor. However, the recently discovered images represent Mictlantecuhtli, 'Lord of the World of the Dead', one of the most highly venerated gods of the Mexicas at the time of the Spaniards' arrival in Mesoamerica (col. pl. 5). In accordance with the religious concepts of the time, Mictlantecuhtli lived on the ninth level of the Underworld, a cold and dark place which was the final destination of all those who died of natural causes. This divinity was represented as a skeletal or partly defleshed being (fig. 11a).

The two sculptures discovered in the tunnels are standing upright and are slightly over life-size. Loincloths and sandals are the only garments that they are wearing. Their heads have dozens of perforations where natural curly hair and bits of paper were inserted, these being natural attributes of the deities of death. The sculptures have prominent ears and stains of yellow paint on the faces, symbolizing putrefaction. Their arms are bent forward with the claws poised for attack. Beneath the thoracic cavity there hang liver sculptures made from the left and right lobes of the liver and the gall bladder (col. pl. 5 and fig 11b). The Mexicas believed that the *ihíyotl*, a soul connected to the Underworld, darkness, the

a   *b*

c   *d*

11 *a) Image of Mictlantecuhtli on a bench (*Códice Magliabechiano, *p. 76r)*
    *b) Mictlantecuhtli with curly hair and liver emerging from his thorax (*Códice Tudela, *p. 52r)*
    *c) Uniform of Tlacochcalcatl with liver emerging from his thorax (*Matrícula de Tributos, *Plate 10)*
    *d) Tzitzímitl with a necklace made of hands and hearts, and with liver emerging from his thorax (*Códice
    Tudela, *p. 40r). (Drawings by Fernando Carrizosa)*

feminine, sexuality and reproduction could be found in this organ (López Austin 1988: 232–6 and personal communication). It is for this reason that not only Mictlantecuhtli, but other deities such as Mictecacíhuatl, Tzitzímitl and Tlacochcalcatl connected with the powers of the lower half of the cosmos, are shown as having enlarged livers (figs 11c and d).

At present we are carrying out an analysis of the materials and the data collected since 1981 with the intention of publishing a complete monograph on the House of Eagles.

Offerings from the sacred precinct of Mexico-Tenochtitlan

Other recent studies have concentrated on the analysis of the rich offerings buried beneath the Templo Mayor as well as in the nearby buildings and squares (fig. 12). This research can be divided into two main aspects. One of them has centred on the economic and political aspects of the Mexica society, to which end the provenance and means of obtaining plants and animals offered to the gods have been studied. Parallel to this, analyses have been made of the origin of the raw materials, manufacturing techniques and styles of the artefacts which served as offerings (López Luján 1994: 128–37).

As far as the origin of the materials from which the offerings were made is concerned, we know that 80 per cent of them are from outside the Basin of Mexico. They come mainly from the territories occupied by the tributary provinces of the Triple Alliance (Tenochtitlan-Texcoco-Tlacopan). The faunal remains are the most abundant; to date more than 200 species have been identified as coming from the temperate ecosystems of the Central Plateau, the tropical jungles, the coral reefs, the estuaries and the coastal lakes. In stark contrast, remains of flora and raw minerals are very scarce. Examples of the former are maguey (a kind of agave), copal incense, coniferous wood and rubber; examples of the latter are marine sand and fragments of jet, turquoise and green stones.

In the sample there is also an ample collection of human bone remains. A few belong to high-ranking individuals who were ritually buried after their bodies had been cremated; the large majority, on the other hand, belong to sacrificial victims who were beheaded or whose throats were cut.

Amongst the retrieved artefacts, it is the imported goods which arrived in Tenochtitlan by means of tribute, commerce, as gifts or through pillaging which stand out: sculptures in the Mixtec style, urns from Veracruz, ceramics and stone artefacts from the Puebla-Tlaxcala region, as well as a large quantity of copper bells and ornaments made of green stones whose origins are

12 *The offerings were excavated and recorded very thoroughly. For example the excavation of Offering U lasted 3 months.* (Photo: Leonardo López Luján, courtesy of INAH)

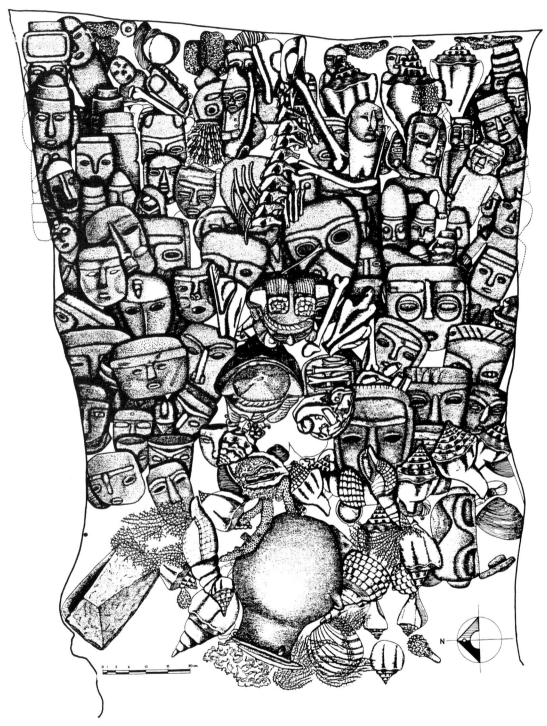

13 *Field drawing of the main level in Chamber 2, one of the richest offerings found in the Great Temple.* (Drawing by Alberto Zúñiga, courtesy of INAH)

not known. Also discovered was an impressive number of antiques unearthed during the fifteenth century from tombs and offerings belonging to societies which were not contemporary with the Mexica: a mask and several fragments of Olmec sculptures; hundreds of masks and figurines in the Mezcala style; dozens of pieces of Teotihuacan stonework and pottery; and a Plumbate ceramic vessel from southeast Mesoamerica. Surprisingly, it is the products of the Mexica themselves which are the most rare.

The second aspect of the research has been directed towards examining the contents and distribution of the offerings with the aim of reaching a better understanding of Mexica ideology. One of the most significant results has been the discovery and recording of the complex arrangement of the archaeological materials within the offering deposits (fig. 13). During the excavation we were able to note that each and every one of the offered objects was placed in a specific position. In fact the offerings were positioned in a way that was not at all haphazard, but followed very clear rules of spatial composition.

In a manner similar to verbal language, each object acted as a sign or symbol which, when combined with other objects, transmitted information. Unfortunately, for nearly two hundred years studies of the Mexica offerings have been limited to the analysis of their contents, thus neglecting their contextual relations. It is precisely for this reason that nowadays we know so much about the significance of many of the individual buried materials, but we still know nothing about the meaning of the whole. Or, to put it another way, we understand the letters and even the words, but not the syntax of the sentences.

With the aim of discovering the greatest number of regularities and deciphering the religious language contained in the offerings, we undertook several analyses of a sample of 8,000 objects belonging to 118 offerings. Initially, and with the aid of simple spatial and statistical techniques,

it was possible to detect two types of archaeological syntax: an 'internal' and an 'external' one.

As far as the internal syntax is concerned, the offered objects were distributed in a particular order within the receptacles, conforming to the following arrangements:

1. The gifts followed imaginary axial lines in a horizontal direction. Those objects which, according to the Mexica world view, had opposing or complementary characters were situated at the ends of the principal axes. For example, in some boxes we found the images of the Fire God and the Rain God in opposed positions.

2. Objects having the same characteristics tended to be grouped together horizontally in units of 5, 9, 13 and 18 components, i.e. numbers relating to the Mexica concept of the cosmos.

3. The objects were placed vertically in levels or layers. Each level consisted of objects of the same kind, following taxonomical criteria which were also based on the indigenous world view. For example, in offering H the top level was made up of ceramics. The next one was occupied by the skeletons of a jaguar and a wolf. A bit further below there was another level which contained sacrificial knives. At the very bottom, on the lowest level, there were objects with an aquatic symbolism.

The offerings were buried in four different types of receptacle:

1. Within the constructional fill (composed of earth and stones), during the process of construction, remodelling or extension of the buildings

2. In large boxes made from carved stones, during the inauguration ceremonies of the temples

3. In recesses dug out beneath the floors, when the buildings were in full use

4. In cube-shaped urns made from volcanic rock (*tepetlacalli*), buried during the construction or inauguration of the building or while it was in use.

Let us look now at the external syntax. Both the position of the offerings and their quality and quantity depended on the importance of the constructions and the semiotic value of each part of the building. We could observe the following patterns:

1. The differential importance of the constructions. Eighty-six offerings were found in the Templo Mayor, compared with only thirty-two offerings found in the neighbouring buildings and squares which were of much less importance.
2. Imaginary axial lines. The offerings were distributed along the principal architectural axes of the buildings.
3. Sculptural monuments. The Mexicas dedicated offerings to monuments incorporated into the architectural structures, such as the sculpture of Coyolxauhqui and the *chac mool* (reclining figure).
4. Horizontal location. The majority of the offering deposits were placed in the east and west facades of the temples, a distribution which has a solar significance.

In addition to the easily detectable regularities, there were others which required more complex statistical techniques to appreciate them. Thanks to the use of methods of numerical classification, taxonomy and spatial analysis, we were able to detect groups of offerings whose content and internal and external syntax were very similar. Some of these offerings were definitely buried at the same time. For example, during the construction of Phase III of the Templo Mayor, six offerings consisting of blue pots and beads made of green stone were buried around Tláloc's shrine (López Luján 1994: 214–23). In this way, the Mexica priests symbolized the water pots of the Rain Gods and positioned them so that they seemed to be pouring precious water onto the Earth's surface. This ceremony was a propitiatory act which conferred on the new building the qualities of the world of Tláloc: a hill from which clouds, rain and consequently the fertility of the land were to be generated. Other offerings, although they were not contemporary, formed part of similar rituals which had the same religious meaning. For example, after death, all individuals of the highest status were cremated and buried with the same type of offerings beneath the stucco floor of the shrine dedicated to Huitzilopochtli (López Luján 1994: 223–40).

Offerings as cosmograms

A considerable number of the offerings retrieved by the Templo Mayor Project were tiny scale models of either sections of the universe or of the complete universe, just as it was conceived by the prehispanic peoples of the Postclassic period. Adhering to a strict liturgy, the Mexica priests took great care in reproducing, with artefacts, animals and plants, the Earth's surface and, occasionally, the different levels of Heaven and the Underworld. It may be said that in this way, during the ritual ceremonies, they were repeating the cosmogonic actions of the gods. In this respect, offering number 16 was one of the most simple and obvious cosmograms (López Luján 1994: 172–92). It was discovered inside a small rectangular platform surrounded by four other platforms which face towards the northeast, the northwest, the southeast and the southwest respectively. Interestingly, the items that made up the offering followed the same spatial distribution as the aforementioned platforms. Found inside a small stone box was an image of Xiuhtecuhtli, 'Lord of the Year' and Fire God, surrounded by five beads of green stone (col. pl. 7). These beads were laid out in a uniform manner in the centre of the box and in the four corners (northeast, northwest, southeast, southwest). A prismatic obsidian knife also lay in the middle. To the east of this box there was a smaller one which was given the number 16-A. Inside there were also five beads made of green stone laid out identically to those in offering number 16: one in the centre and one in each corner.

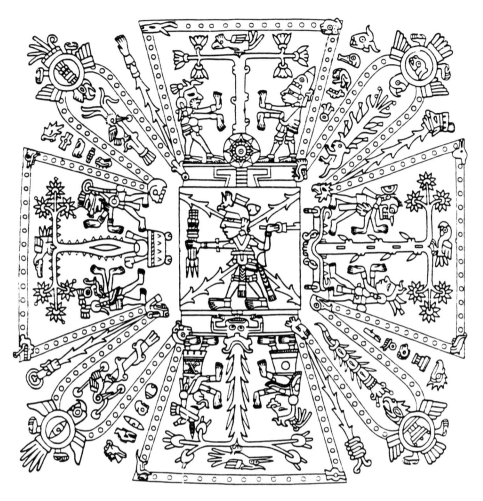

14 *Plate 1 of the* Códice Fejérváry-Mayer *represents the five regions of the earth's surface. The central rectangle – the centre of the universe – is occupied by Xiuhtecuhtli, the Fire God.*

The particular distribution of the five architectural platforms and the five groups of beads represents the *quincunx*, the Mesoamerican symbol of the five regions that make up the Earth's surface (the four cardinal points and the Earth's centre). The image of Xiuhtecuhtli alludes to an extremely important deity who, according to sixteenth-century sources, lived at the centre of the universe. Xiuhtecuhtli was the Fire God in relation to the four cardinal points, just like the brazier that occupied the centre of each house and temple. For this reason he was invoked as *Tlalxictenticaé,*

Nauhiotecatlé, that is, 'He who is filling the navel of the Earth, He of the Group of Four' (Sahagún 1988: 545). This idea is shown, among other places, in plate I of the *Códice Fejérváry-Mayer* (1994). I am referring to the representation of the universe which integrates the principles of the organization of time and space (fig. 14). In it can be observed the four directions of the universe occupied by the cosmic trees and the Lords of the Night. In the central box, the navel of the world, is Xiuhtecuhtli.

The dual offerings: Water and Fire in the Templo Mayor of Tenochtitlan

We will go on to see an interesting group of offerings which are characterized by a dual meaning which conforms with the double pattern of the Templo Mayor. With regard to this, let us remember that several indigenous myths indicate that double geographical accidents revealed to the Mexicas the site for erecting their Templo Mayor: two caves (Alvarado Tezozómoc 1949: 62–3) or two crags from which flowed two streams, one with blue water, the other with red water (Durán 1984: 44). Later, these two colours and their insistent duality would contribute their distinctive themes to the temples of Huitzilopochtli and Tláloc, and to the offerings buried there.

The eleven offerings that we will analyse were buried at Stage IVb of the Templo Mayor, i.e. around about AD 1469 (López Luján 1994: 240–98). Their distribution follows the principal architectural axes of the platform and observes a strict bilateral symmetry. Thanks to archaeological records, it is easy to prove that the eleven offerings formed part of the inauguration rituals whose aim was to repeat the divine act of creation and reproduce the universe to scale. Inside each offering box the objects were found to form six levels which reproduce to scale the three planes of the indigenous universe:

1. The deepest, having aquatic characteristics.
2. The middle plane, which had an earthly significance.
3. The highest, which was presided over by the Fire and Water Gods, and in which stand out the symbols of opposing and complementary natures, the insignias of Xipe Tótec and the skulls of decapitated human beings (fig. 15).

To start off with, those making the offerings placed a layer of marine sand at the bottom of each box. It is very plausible that this layer was meant to represent symbolically that part of the universe having aquatic characteristics: the Tlalocan or

Xalli itepeuhyan ('spillway of sand'). The priest went on to create a second level with small snails and small seashells, and immediately on top a third layer made up of corals and larger snails. In relation to the meaning of these levels we should point out that the Mexicas saw marine animals as cold, damp beings coming from the Underworld. What is more, the snail was compared with the female womb and consequently acted as a symbol of fertility.

The fourth level was made up exclusively of the remains of fish and reptiles. However, those making the offerings only placed in them the external parts of these animals: the heads and skins of crocodiles and snakes; the heads and scales of fish; the cartilage of sawfish; the shells of turtles. Most of the fish lacked their spines and were represented by heads, skins and fins. The original image of this level would be that of a 'layer of skin' which physically and visually separated the deeper aquatic levels from the upper one. In my opinion, this intermediate level can be connected to Cipactli, the female sea monster which symbolized the Earth. It is sufficient to recall that Cipactli was represented iconographically by a crocodile, a sawfish or a snake.

The fifth level was the richest of all. It was made up of the images of gods, miniatures of divine paraphernalia, instruments for self-sacrifice and the skulls of beheaded individuals. Of all these objects it is the images of Xiuhtecuhtli (the Fire God) and Tláloc (the Rain God) which stand out. Both were always found at the top of the deposit, dominating the offering, and they were distributed in a regular fashion around the Templo Mayor. Three objects of divine paraphernalia also appeared recurrently: a sceptre in the shape of the head of a deer, the symbol of the sun, fire and drought; a sceptre in the shape of a snake connected with the currents of water and the fertilizing rays; and a *chicahuaztli*, the sceptre of the god Xipe Tótec. There were likewise a number of human skulls with cervical vertebrae included. It is worth mentioning that to date there are fifty-

15 *Main level of Offering 61 in the Great Temple, dominated by the images of the Fire God and the Rain God.* (Photo: Salvador Guilliem, courtesy of INAH)

six of these skulls, discovered in the corners and principal axes of the building.

The sixth and last level was found just above the stone slabs that covered the offering boxes. It was made up of ceramic censers which were ritually 'killed'.

One of the main keys to the meaning of this group is found in the presence of the skulls of beheaded individuals. As is well known, the religious custom of severing the head from the body dates back to the earliest times of Mesoamerica. Broadly speaking, it may be said that the peoples of Ancient Mexico associated the human head with the *tonalli* (soul), corn and the sun, and they practised ritual beheading at ceremonies which generally emphasized binary opposition: the ball game, the ritual of sowing and harvesting, the sacrifice of prisoners of war to renew the *tzompantli* (skull rack) and the consecration of the temples.

In relation to the last type of ceremony, many skulls with cervical vertebrae attached have been found in the corners of a number of religious structures dating from the Middle Preclassic period to the Late Postclassic period, from the Maya area right up to the Tarascan plateau. These findings are corroborated by indigenous pictography, in which it is not difficult to find representations of offerings of decapitated heads inside temples. At the beginning of the sixteenth century, the Nahua people and the Maya believed that the recently completed building received the 'soul' through the sacrifice and burial of a human being beneath its foundations.

But let us return to Tenochtitlan. Fortunately, the burial of the decapitated heads in the offerings of the Templo Mayor was recorded in sixteenth-century sources. The Mexicas offered heads on the occasion of the inauguration of the extension of the main temple, a festival which always took place in *Tlacaxipehualiztli*, the month dedicated to the god Xipe Tótec. Sahagún mentions that during this festival war captives were sacrificed by having their hearts extracted and that afterwards

their bodies were decapitated. Later, the warriors would dance for hours, holding the severed heads of their captives. Finally, according to Alva Ixtlilxóchitl (1975: 157), the heads were 'fitted into recesses specially made in the walls of the Templo Mayor', an obvious reference to the offering boxes.

It is extremely important that, as recorded in the colonial documents of the Crónica X tradition, *all* the inauguration ceremonies of the Templo Mayor took place at the same time of the year: during the month of Xipe Tótec. This month coincided with the spring equinox, the balancing point between day and night. Unfortunately, ever since Seler (1899) suggested for the first time that such a festival alluded to the spring renewal of vegetation, this idea has been unquestioningly reproduced over and over again. As Nicholson (1972) affirms, Seler's hypothesis is no more than a typical construction of Western logic which is completely lacking in proof.

By contrast, the sense of *Tlacaxipehualiztli* would seem rather to be connected to war, the creation of the Fifth Sun and the balancing of opposites. In agreement with Nicholson (1972), *Tlacaxipehualiztli* could be connected to the acquisition of war trophies. This idea is in keeping with the gloss in the *Códice Vaticano-Latino 3738* (1964–7: pl. X and p.30) which attributes to Xipe Tótec the creation of war and the fact that the Mexica kings attired themselves to resemble this god during battle.

According to Graulich (1982), the ceremonies of *Tlacaxipehualiztli* were directly related to war (the joining of opposites), and with the birth of the Sun and with the harvest. After a detailed analysis of the myths and rituals, this author concludes that the festival re-enacted the myth of the origin of the Fifth Sun and the first war. It would refer to that moment when, after the world had been created and destroyed on four occasions, the gods met at Teotihuacan to undertake the fifth attempt, the definitive one. After rising above the horizon, the Sun ordered the massacre of 400 *mimixcoah* so that it could begin its daily movement. This is extremely interesting, since in this way the inauguration ceremony of the Templo Mayor and the burial of cosmogram offerings would have the intention of recreating the first act of the creation of the universe with the aim of ensuring its reality and longevity. Consecrating the temple signifies recreating the universe and time.

According to Kurath and Martí (1964), the rituals of *Tlacaxipehualiztli* represent the conflicts between Heaven and Earth, light and darkness, and the dry and rainy seasons. From this perspective it seems logical that the festival celebrating the consecration of this double temple dedicated to a solar deity and a water deity should take place during a month associated with the balancing of opposites. Discoveries by Tichy (1981) and Ponce de León (1982) support this idea. Both researchers, when calculating the orientation of the Templo Mayor, found that the

sun rose exactly between the shrine of Huitzilopochtli and that of Tláloc on the 4th March each year, i.e. on the first day of the month of *Tlacaxipehualiztli*. This is revealing because, according to Tichy, the orientation of the prehispanic temples might indicate the first day of the festival of the god to which they were dedicated (fig. 16).

We should also add that in an offering belonging to this same group, Guzmán Camacho (1997) discovered that the fish which were buried there had been captured between the months of February and April.

I wish to refer to the political aspect of the events in *Tlacaxipehualiztli*. This aspect is apparent in the documents of the Crónica X Tradition. All inaugurations mentioned therein follow the same sequence of events:

1. Almost at the end of the work on the extension an expedition would be organized to conquer

16 *On the first day of the month of Tlacaxipehualiztli the sun rose between the two shrines of the Great Temple.* (Courtesy of the Mesoamerican Archive Research Project, Princeton University)

an independent domain in order to obtain prisoners destined to be sacrificed for the consecration of the Templo Mayor.

2. After the victorious return of the Mexica armies there would be a wait until the month of *Tlacaxipehualiztli*.

3. Governors of allied domains hostile to the Triple Alliance would be invited to the event.

4. During the festivities compatriots of the enemy lords invited would be sacrificed and their heads buried in the corners of the Templo Mayor.

A careful reading of these documents reveals an important fact: the Templo Mayor grew in relation to the growth of the empire. In this way, its various successive extensions glorified the military expansion and acted as ideological justification of the imperial politics. Each extension symbolized, celebrated and sanctified the inclusion of new tributaries within the Mexica domain. In circumstances where the armies of the Triple Alliance could not conquer an independent domain – such as the fruitless expedition to Michoacán – the inauguration would be postponed until a conquest could be made. This helps us to understand why the Templo Mayor increased in size at least twelve times in 130 years.

In conclusion, both the architectural configuration and the offerings of the Templo Mayor represented a scale model of the universe as it was conceived by the Mexicas. Each extension involved ceremonies in which the cosmogonic actions of the gods were repeated and the Underworld, the Heavens and the Earth were recreated. At the same time, the temple and the offerings provided a symbolic synthesis of the two basic aspects, opposed and complementary, of the Mexica religion: Fire and Water, elements whose union (*atl-tlachinolli*, 'water-blaze') was a metaphor for the cosmic war.

References

Alva Ixtlilxóchitl, Fernando de (1975) *Obras históricas*, 2 vols. México: UNAM.

Alvarado Tezozómoc, Hernando (1949) *Crónica mexicáyotl*. México: UNAM-INAH.

Beyer, Hermann (1940) 'El jeroglífico de Tlacaélel', *Revista Mexicana de Estudios Antropológicos*, vol. IV, 161–4.

Boone, Elizabeth H. (1987) 'Templo Mayor Research, 1521-1978', *The Aztec Templo Mayor*, E.H. Boone (ed.), 5–70. Washington, DC: Dumbarton Oaks.

Broda, Johanna, Davíd Carrasco and Eduardo Matos Moctezuma (1987) *The Great Temple of Tenochtitlan. Center and Periphery in the Aztec World*. Berkeley: University of California Press.

Códice Fejérváry-Mayer (1994) México: Fondo de Cultura Económica/Akademische Druck- und Verlagsanstalt.

Códice Vaticano-Latino 3738 (1964–7) Lord Kingsborough, *Antigüedades de México*. México: Secretaría de Hacienda y Crédito Público, III, 7–314.

Durán, Diego (1984) *Historia de las Indias de Nueva España e Islas de la Tierra Firme*, 2 vols. México: Porrúa.

Fuente, Beatriz de la (1990) 'Escultura en el tiempo. Retorno al pasado tolteca', *Artes de México*, nueva época, 9, 36–53.

Graulich, Michel (1982) 'Tlacaxipehualiztli ou la fête aztèque de la moisson et de la guerre', *Revista española de estudios antropológicos*, XII, 215–54.

Gutiérrez Solana, Nelly (1989) 'Diez años de estudios sobre el Templo Mayor de Tenochtitlan', *Anales del Instituto de Investigaciones Estéticas*, 60, 7–31.

Guzmán Camacho, Ana Fabiola (1997) 'Análisis arqueoictiológico de la Ofrenda 23 del Templo Mayor de Tenochtitlan'. Tesis de Maestría en Biología. México: Instituto Politécnico Nacional, Escuela Nacional de Ciencias Biológicas.

Klein, Cecilia F. (1987) 'The Ideology of Autosacrifice at the Templo Mayor', *The Aztec Templo Mayor*, E.H. Boone (ed), 293–370. Washington, DC: Dumbarton Oaks.

Kurath, Gertrude y Samuel Martí (1964) *Dances of*

Anahuac: The Choreography and Music of Precortesian Dances. Chicago: Aldine.

León-Portilla, Miguel (1987) 'The Ethnohistorical Record for the Huey Teocalli of Tenochtitlan', *The Aztec Templo Mayor*, E.C. Boone (ed), 71–96. Washington DC: Dumbarton Oaks.

López Austin, Alfredo (1988) *Human Body and Ideology. Concepts of the Ancient Nahuas*, 2 vols. Salt Lake City: University of Utah Press.

López Luján, Leonardo (1989) 'Ausgrabungen in Tlatelolco (Mexiko)', *Das Altertum*, vol. 35, no. 4, 249–53.

López Luján, Leonardo (1994) *The Offerings of the Templo Mayor of Tenochtitlan*. Niwot: University Press of Colorado.

López Luján, Leonardo (1995) 'Guerra y muerte en Tenochtitlan. Descubrimientos en el Recinto de los Guerreros Aguila', *Arqueología mexicana*, II, 12, 75–7.

López Luján, Leonardo and Vida Mercado (1996) 'Dos esculturas de Mictlantecuhtli encontradas en el Recinto Sagrado de Mexico-Tenochtitlan', *Estudios de Cultura Náhuatl*, 26, 41–68.

Matos Moctezuma, Eduardo (1988) *The Great Temple of the Aztecs. Treasures of Tenochtitlan*. London: Thames and Hudson.

Matos Moctezuma, Eduardo and Leonardo López Luján (1993) 'Teotihuacan and its Mexica Legacy', *Teotihuacan, Art from the City of the Gods*, K. Berrin and E. Pasztory (eds), 156–65. San Francisco: Thames and Hudson/The Fine Arts Museums of San Francisco.

Matrícula de Tributos. Nuevos estudios (1991) México: Secretaría de Hacienda y Crédito Público.

Nicholson, H.B. (1972) 'The Cult of Xipe Tótec in Mesoamerica', *Religión en Mesoamérica, XII Mesa Redonda*, 213–18. México: Sociedad Mexicana de Antropología.

Ortiz, Agustín, Luis Barba, Leonardo López Luján, Karl F. Link and Luz Lazos (1996) 'Chemical analysis of Residues in Floors and the Reconstruction of Ritual Activities at Templo Mayor', *Archaeological Chemistry. Organic, Inorganic and Biochemical Analysis* (ACS Symposium Series 625), V. Orna (ed.). Washington, DC: American Chemical Society .

Ponce de León, Arturo (1982) *Fechamiento arqueoastronómico en el Altiplano de México*. México: Departamento del Distrito Federal.

Rojas, José Luis (1992) *México-Tenochtitlan. Economía y sociedad en el siglo XVI*. México: El Colegio de Michoacán/Fondo de Cultura Económica.

Sahagún, Bernardino de (1988) *Historia general de las cosas de Nueva España*, 2 vols. Madrid: Alianza Editorial.

Seler, Eduard (1899) 'Die achtzehn Jahresfeste der Mexikaner (1 Hälfte)', *Veröffentlichungen aus dem Königlichen Museum für Völkerkunde*, Berlin, 6, 58–66.

Tichy, Franz (1981) 'Order and Relationship of Space and Time in Mesoamerica: Myth or Reality', *Mesoamerican Sites and World-views*, E.P. Benson (ed.), 217–45. Washington DC: Dumbarton Oaks.

3. Place Signs in Mesoamerican Inscriptions and Codices

Gordon Brotherston

Along with calendrical and chronological signs, place signs (toponyms) constitute a main element in what has been called the 'Mixtec-Aztec' or iconic script of Mesoamerica. Based on standard images such as mountain, river, tree, wall, field, ball court, shrine, house, these place signs are readily recognizable in otherwise obscure contexts. They first appear before 500 BC in Olmec inscriptions and then abound at Preclassic Monte Albán. They are a dominant feature of the pre- and post-Conquest books of paper and deerskin known as *codices*, and of cotton *lienzo* maps; they also appear in the *Relaciones Geográficas* of 1580, and through the medium of the Landbooks (*Techialoyan*) were accepted as legal evidence during the whole of the Spanish colonial period. Today they are still visible in the logos used by transport companies, the blue road signs of the State of Mexico, and the emblems of Mexico City's subway stations.[1]

Incorporated in various ways into the phonetic scripts developed by the Olmec and the lowland Maya, these standardized visual signs can be read simultaneously in the different languages of Mesoamerica, Zapotec, Mixe, Mixtec, Chocho, Náhuatl, Totonac, Otomí and so on. The mountain or pyramid sign transcribed as *tepetl* in Náhuatl (the term adopted here) is *yucu* in Mixtec (fig. 17), while river is respectively *apan* and *yuta*. In the Coixtlahuaca Lienzo 1 (Seler Lienzo 2), the surrounding toponymic frame is glossed in no less than three languages, Náhuatl, Chocho and Mixtec, each proper to the regional culture in question (König 1984). In other cases, where a

place name differs between languages, glyphs may represent both readings, for example the Náhuatl and Totonac names for Xicotepec in the Xicotepec Annals (Stresser-Péan 1995: 9) or the Náhuatl and Chocho names for Matlatlan (Maltrata) in Cholula and Coixtlahuaca texts (Brotherston 1995a: 73) (fig. 18). On the whole question of phoneticism, it is worth recalling that it was known as a principle in Mesoamerica for two millennia before Cortés, and that it is misleading to suggest, as some have done, that on the eve of the European invasion the area was somehow on the brink of a 'phonetic breakthrough'. Rather, texts like the Tepetlaoztoc Codex indicate that the sounds of Náhuatl place names could be quite adequately represented in script, but that for political reasons this practice was restricted to smaller and local subject towns (col. pl. 8).[2] In practice, not being tied to the sounds of one or other speech enabled Mesoamerican toponyms not just to be read internationally but, over time, to survive the imposition of successive empires. With reference to the *lienzos*, Marcus (1992: 171) notes how a 'prehispanic place sign appears to have persisted longer in its function as a boundary marker than it did as the name of a town'.

While the occurrence of place signs in the codices has been widely recognized,[3] less has been said so far about those found in cities throughout Mesoamerica, most often at far earlier dates, inscribed on stone, jade and bone, painted on plaster, and wrought in gold. Salient examples occur at Monte Albán and Xochicalco; others have been recently unearthed at Cacaxtla and

Inscriptions:

Codices:

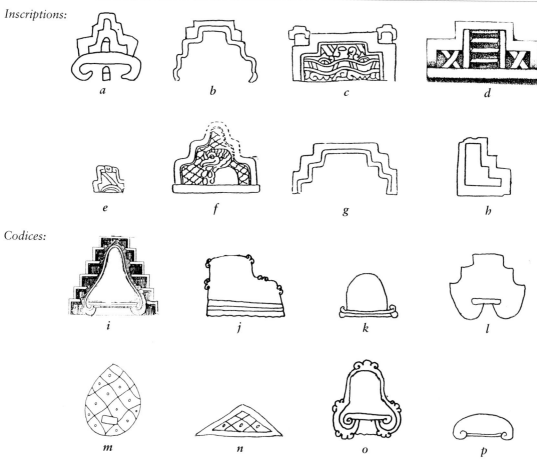

17 Tepetl *types.*
a) Ahuelican greenstone; b) Stela, Museo Regional Oaxaca; c) Monolith South Platform, Monte Albán; d) Tequixtepec Stone V (Ñuiñe); e) Pacific Coast; f) Cacaxtla; g) Stela 2-C, Xochicalco; h) Stone 10, Xochicalco. After Coe, Diehl et al. 1995; Urcid 1993, 1994; Moser 1977; Marcus 1980.
i) Guevea Lienzo; j) Tepexic Annals (Vienna); k) Miltepec Roll (Baranda); l) Cuauhtinchan Map 1; m) Tochpan Lienzos; n) Xolotl Maps; o) Tlapiltepec Lienzo; p) Azcapotzalco Techialoyan (García Granados).

18 *Double place glyphs.*
a) bee (Xicotepec) and old man (Kakolun), Xicotepec Annals p.9; b) net (Matlatlan) and tree, Tlapiltepec Lienzo – net on tree-trunk, Miltepec Roll (Baranda) – net in tree roots, Cuauhtinchan Map 1.

19 *Toponyms on Building J, Monte Albán.*
1. Cuicatlan (singer, rattle); 2. Tochtepec (rabbit); 3. Coyolapan (bell, bead; river); 4. Zaachila (?reed); 5. Miahuatlan (maize flower); 6. Tututepec (bird); 7. Tehuantepec (carnivore); 8. Aztlatlan (heron).
a1-8 Building J (1, 5-7 after Marcus 1980; 6 after Marcus 1992); b4, 7 Guevea Lienzo (after Seler); c1, 6 Nuttall pp.73, 45; d1 Vienna p.8; d6 Colombino p.4; e1-3, 7 Mendoza ff.43, 46, 44, 13v (after Berdan and Anawalt 1992); e5, 6 Telleriano ff.41, 40v (after Quiñones 1995); f5, 7 Tlaxcala Lienzo (Glasgow version) pp.143, 152.

Teotihuacan. These sources demand comparison with the codices, particularly the encyclopaedic account of Aztec Tenochtitlan's tribute empire known as the Mendoza Codex (Berdan and Anawalt 1992), a comparison which can be highly informative, as pioneering studies by Seler (1904b), Marcus (1980) and others show. True, many technical and other difficulties impede this comparison, for example the poor restoration of the inscribed texts or the simple fact that these are often read in the reverse direction to that imposed by Western numbering. Yet significant advances have been made in recent years especially with regard to defining the potential of toponyms as elements of Mesoamerican script. The earliest surviving examples of place glyphs may have had their origin in the design of empire, yet for native communities today they continue to have a key function in the defence of lands (see note 1, p.65).

Monte Albán

Following their first appearance before 500 BC in Olmec inscriptions, from about 100 BC toponymic glyphs become a major feature of the script used at Monte Albán (the Zapotec capital in Oaxaca) and surrounding valleys, which was later extended north to Cuicatlan and the Ñuiñe area (Huajuapan-Tequixtepec) and south to Tututepec. At Monte Albán itself these glyphs are most numerous at the southern end of the main plaza, on the faces of the southern platform, on monoliths and stelae, and above all on Building J (fig. 19).

The place sign characteristic of Monte Albán is a pyramid or temple platform depicted in outline or profile which rises through two or three levels. As a constructed object this design may include a frontal stairway, read by some as a specific reference to Cholula ('the place of stairs' in Mixtec), and frequently serves as the base for jaguar-conquerors, framing the cast-down heads of their defeated foes; in one case, the pyramid is delivered by hand as a conquered object. Following Olmec precedent, some versions of the design include more rounded matching inner forms, even the image of protruding earth as a saurian head with eyes and cave mouth, and hence bring out the analogy in principle between the hard-edged pyramid and the natural mountain which it imitates, both of them called *tepetl* in Náhuatl. The play in principle between natural and constructed forms in toponyms is one found likewise in the codices, a notable example being the Tepotzotlan Codex which deliberately alternates five landscape features with five buildings (Brotherston 1995a: 174–5). The stepped form specific to the *tepetl* of Monte Albán was later imitated beyond the bounds of its empire, in the Ñuiñe area (Moser 1977) and at Xochicalco, Cacaxtla and Cuauhtinchan (figs 17a–i). Inset into it we then find the locative elements of particular place names, conventionalized in a fashion similar to that of Mesoamerican calendar signs.

The toponyms clustered on Building J belong to Monte Albán II, that is, they were carved in the Protoclassic between 100 BC and AD 200, on the smoothed faces of large and small slabs which were subsequently incorporated into the main structure. The modern restoration of this building is evidently imperfect; certain of the fifty or more known incised slabs can be seen lying nearby while others are now stored in museums. Even so, much can be learned from this early geopolitical statement at Monte Albán.

A constant feature of Building J toponyms is the *tepetl* glyph, below which hangs the inverted head of a defeated ruler, distinguished by type of headdress and facial marking. Variable signs then indicate particular places, shown to be conquests by arrows, the fingerboard of a spear-thrower, grasping hands and other recurrent affixes. Recognizable among the place signs already at this early stage are both natural features such as river (in cross section), tree, fauna (e.g. insect, rabbit, jaguar, bird) and body parts, and also 'artificial' features such as flag, house or temple, and fortified wall. Of interest is the link with Olmec convention in such elements as the diagonal cross-band, and the trilobe (La Venta, Monument 13; also seen as a roar emitted by jaguars at Teotihuacan). There is also a key link with the Olmec in the overall equivalence established between the face and body of humans and other vertebrates and that of the earth itself, whereby head is hill, nose is promontory, teeth are bricks in a wall, mouth and nostrils arc caves, hair is vegetation. In this respect, certain of the Monte Albán toponyms closely correspond to those inscribed on the Olmec jades and greenstone found at Ahuelican (Guerrero), Cantona and Tepoztlan, even in numerical detail. Most striking is the fact that the Ahuelican example, which is extremely early (900–500 BC) anticipates the play at Monte Albán between the human face and the face of the earth at the same time as it establishes the analogy between the *tepetl* as both natural mountain and human construct (figs 17a and 20).[4]

Besides setting up iconic conventions in this way, the Building J toponyms also establish a definite reading pattern. For, beginning in the southeast, they read from right to left in two principal registers, the upper one including the lintels of a passage that runs through the western end of the building. Despite the problems of restoration, it seems likely that the total of toponyms in each of the upper and the lower sequences matches that of the steps in the main stairway, that is twice eleven (4+7), a ritually significant number. At the same time, it has been suggested that, given its odd alignment and the asymmetrical wedge shape of its inscribed faces, the building might represent Monte Albán's actual frontiers, a model of empire, but too much has now been lost for this to be proven.

Following Alfonso Caso (1965), who first excavated the site, Joyce Marcus (1980, 1992) made a concerted effort to interpret the Monte

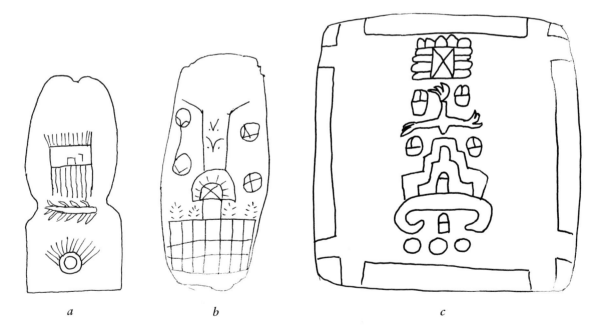

a   *b*   *c*

20 *Olmec jade and greenstone.*
a) Cantona; b) Tlacotenco, Tepoztlan; c) Ahuelican. In b) and c) there are nostril and mouth elements while the four seed-eyes recall the fact that the eye is literally the 'seed of the face' in proto-Mixe-Zoque (L. Schele, quoted in Coe, Diehl et al. 1995: 230).

Albán toponyms and to relate them to those found in the codices. She starts from the premise that Monte Albán was a politically conscious centre, with diplomatic relations that reached to Teotihuacan and beyond, and which resulted in detailed statements of conquest. Identifying and discussing the constituent elements of the toponyms, she places them in the longer story of Zapotec writing represented in the sixteenth century by the Guevea Lienzo. Where appropriate she then compares particular toponyms with those included in the tribute lists of Tenochtitlan, which was carrying forward the same history of empire when Cortés arrived.

Hence, the place with a singer glyph is identified as Cuicatlan, an ancient town which had immense strategic significance for Monte Albán as it later did for Aztec Tenochtitlan. As modern archaeology has shown,[5] Cuicatlan marked the northern limit of Protoclassic Monte Albán's power, a key to the great east–west trade route that ran through the Tehuacán-Papaloapan valley, past Coixtlahuaca and Tochtepec; according to the Mendoza Codex (f.7v), it was the capture of Coixtlahuaca that opened to Tenochtitlan the unparalleled wealth of the Lower Papaloapan and the east generally. Some of the intervening detail of Cuicatlan's story can be gleaned from the annals of Teozacoalco, Tilantongo and other Mixtec towns that report the ruler Eight Deer's dealings with ruler Four Jaguar of Coixtlahauca early in the eleventh century, as well as the *lienzos* and scrolls of the Coixtlahauca Valley which place Cuicatlan alongside their own federal emblem, and the little-studied annals of Quiotepec and Cuicatlan itself. In the versions of the Cuicatlan glyph that appear in the Mixtec annals of Teozacoalco (Codex Nuttall; Jansen 1992a) and Tepexic (Codex Vienna; Jansen 1992b), though not in that of the Mendoza Codex, the singer also has a rattle and drum. Given the proven links between Monte Albán and the Papaloapan trade route, the question arises whether or not we should go on to find an allusion to the great commercial centre of Tochtepec (Tuxtepec) in a near-contiguous glyph in Building J which Marcus has characterized as the 'hill of the Rabbit' (*tochtli* = rabbit in Náhuatl). In the Mendoza Codex, the tribute district of Tochtepec adjoins that of Coixtlahuaca, to which Cuicatlan belongs, and Bradomín (1992) notes that the local Chinantec name for Tuxtepec contains a rabbit element. Here, however, direct archaeological underpinning is lacking.

The other limit of Monte Albán's power was the southern sea, the province successfully invaded by Eight Deer and named Yucusaa or Tututepec ('bird hill') in the Mixtec Annals. The Texcoco historian Ixtlilxochitl refers to the antiquity and cultural complexity of this coastal area and tells how the Toltecs established a trading colony there that issued copper axe-monies, similar to those once used as far away as the Pacific coast of Ecuador and Peru.[6] As at Cuicatlan, Monte Albán's presence at Tututepec has also been corroborated by archaeology and the study of an extensive repertoire of stelae (Urcid 1993). The bird glyph of Yucusaa/Tututepec, the same as that used in the Mixtec Annals, is apparent enough in the Monte Albán inscriptions and is discussed by Marcus. She, however, makes the visual comparison with a bird glyph in the Mendoza Codex which denotes a different Tututepec (1992: 176); in the Mexica texts, the actual glyph for the Oaxacan Tututepec is registered in the Telleriano Codex, apropos of Moctezuma's attack of 1513 (f.43; Quiñones 1995).

Besides Cuicatlan and Tututepec, Marcus's 1980 study suggests two further comparisons between toponyms on Monte Albán Building J and those in the Mendoza Codex, the latter being Miahuatlan and Ocelotepec (f.52). The Monte Albán flowering maize glyph (especially the riverless version added in Marcus 1992) indeed well matches the flowering maize of Miahuatlan in Mendoza; yet, as with Tututepec, the town in this Mexica (Aztec) source lies in quite a different area (Tochpan). The Miahuatlan of Oaxaca, well to the south of Monte Albán but inland from the coastal mountains, never became a Mexica tributary, although the Telleriano Codex claims that it was attacked by Moctezuma in 1503 (f.41). Along with a great range of other towns that lay beyond Tenochtitlan's grasp, this Miahuatlan appears as a definite Tlaxcalan-Spanish conquest in the Tlaxcala Lienzo (Glasgow version; Acuña 1982–8, 4: 143).

The case of the 'jaguar' town Ocelotepec is similar, insofar as the Mendoza glyph quoted by Marcus again belongs to territory far from Oaxaca; yet it is more complex, since although the Oaxacan Ocelotepec named by Marcus was known as tributary, it is absent from the Mendoza Codex and no glyph at all has survived for it. At the same time, the glyph of another, and far better known, Oaxacan town exactly corresponds to this jaguar glyph on Building J, that of Tehuantepec, the eastern capital of the Zapotecs. Oddly overlooked in previous studies, this glyph features prominently in such Zapotec sources as the Guevea Lienzo mentioned by Marcus and the *Relación geográfica* of Tehuantepec (Acuña 1982–8, 3: 126), as well as in Mendoza (f.13v), Telleriano (f.41) and the Tlaxcala Lienzo (p.152). It consists precisely of a jaguar head, 'jaguar' town being the name of this place in Zapotec, Mixe and Mixtec (Bradomín 1992: 234–5), while in Náhuatl it denotes the carnivorous *tecuani* (Tehuantepec derives from Tecuantepec). Marcus actually describes the appearance of this 'fierce feline' in the Guevea Lienzo, although in another context and without making the link back to Monte Albán (1992: 73).

Just as Cuicatlan and Tututepec establish northern and southwestern limits for Monte Albán's power, so Tehuantepec establishes a boundary to the southeast, which is abundantly confirmed on linguistic, cultural and archae-ological grounds (Monte Albán II is otherwise present at Tehuantepec). This opening to the east has hitherto not been recognized so explicitly in native script. Once entertained, it could help with the decoding of the heron-like bird's head in another of the Building J toponyms, since an ancient neighbouring settlement, the 'heron' place Aztlatlan (Astata), is denoted by a similar glyph in the Tehuantepec Lienzo (*Lienzo de Tecciztepec y Tequatepec*, in Glass 1964).

The perfect match between the Monte Albán jaguar toponym and the glyph for the eastern Zapotec capital Tehuantepec shown in the Guevea Lienzo leads us next to re-examine the glyph for the western capital shown in this same Lienzo, Zaachila, a great archaeological centre that lies just to the south of Monte Albán. The very form of Zaachila's *tepetl* sign in the Lienzo reminds us of this proximity since it replicates the characteristic Monte Albán play between outer artificial pyramid and inner natural mountain (figs 17a, l and 19). Inset into the Zaachila *tepetl* is a crown-like element, listed in Moser's Dictionary of Ñuiñe motifs (1977: 120, no. 60), which he and other scholars have repeatedly noted among the glyphs on Building J itself, albeit without making the link to the Guevea Lienzo. Unmistakable in this source, it further illuminates the geopolitics of the Building J text by affirming the centre, the Zapotec capital Zaachila, later matched in the east by Tehuantepec.

Here references to Mendoza Codex and Náhuatl sources are of less use since in that language Zaachila became the quite different Teozapotlan (Telleriano f.40v). Further, for their tribute capital in this area the Mexica chose Coyolapan (Cuilapan), the river of the bell (Mendoza f.44), which lies between Zaachila and Monte Albán. For its part, however, this town may just be present in Building J, as a river above which we see a round pendant on a necklace, of the type which carries bells in the Xaltepec Annals (p.10; Caso 1964) and the Tlaxcala Lienzo (p.121); Monte Albán II is certainly present at the site. More critically, the Mixtec name for this place denotes a necklace of *quacoyul* beads, which are jet-black and round (Bradomín 1992: 15), it being the case that the gold bells seen in the Mixtec and Náhuatl sources post-date the carving of the

Monte Albán II glyph on Building J.

In all, this series of comparisons between toponyms on Building J and in the codices, begun by Joyce Marcus, has led to the identifying of as many as eight of them, establishing limits of political control to centre, southwest, north and east which correspond to archaeological evidence, and which from that great distance in time prefigure the boundaries of modern Oaxaca. The persistence through time of the glyphs for Cuicatlan (Marcus), Tehuantepec and Zaachila – the least disputable – of itself establishes for Mesoamerica a principle of continuity over many centuries not just in iconography but in geopolitics.

Xochicalco

A major political centre in the late Classic period, Xochicalco also reported on its dominion in several inscribed texts. These use a variety of *tepetl* forms, some reminiscent of Monte Albán, and include a rich array of specific place elements. Toponyms appear on several stelae, the Palace Stone and other panels, and above all on the Plumed Serpent Pyramid (PSP). Housed in the Cuernavaca Museum under the name 'Piedra Coatlan', the Palace Stone includes not just toponyms but linking footprint roads (a feature found already in Olmec inscriptions), and in this directly anticipates codex-type maps. The question of its provenance and focus has been troubled by contradictory readings of its principal glyph, thought by some to be a snake and by others to be a bird.

As a complex text and potential model of empire, the text on the four sides of the Pyramid readily compares with that on Monte Albán's Building J. Though imperfect and in part imperfectly restored, it can be seen to register levels of conquest, rising from the elegant and elaborately dated Olmec-Maya sequence at the base to that of the square shield bearers in the frieze above them (Sequence 2) and then, on the face of the superstructure, to that of the arrow-wielding wearers of wide-brimmed hats (Sequence 3). Starting at the middle of the rear eastern wall, Sequence 2 runs westwards in parallel streams along both north and south walls culminating in the main west-facing stairway; starting here in the west, Sequence 3 then returns, also in parallel, to the middle of the rear eastern wall.

Today over half the toponyms in Sequences 2 and 3 are missing, yet still there is much to be decoded (fig. 21). Seler (1904a) offered his reading a century ago and made line drawings clearer than any others published since. Seler also anticipated the two lines of enquiry taken up by his successors, which have diverged often to their mutual detriment: the astronomical, well defended by Morante (1993); and the material-historical, advanced by Hirth (1989), which has led to direct comparisons with Mexica subject towns listed in the Mendoza Codex, as well as hypothetical identifications with places for which no glyphs have otherwise survived. The range of Hirth's suggestions, which includes subjects of the Mexica tribute centre Huaxtepec in eastern Morelos, is useful in establishing in principle the size of Xochicalco's domain.

A main help in the interpretation of the Xochicalco texts is the Coatlan Map (*Reedificación de Cuernavaca Codex*; Arana 1990), functionally a counterpart to the Guevea Lienzo: both documents are post-Conquest and defend political interests that have their roots in major cities of the past (Xochicalco, Monte Albán), and add glosses (in Náhuatl and Zapotec) to their array of place signs. As heir to Xochicalco's central domain, Coatlan laid claim to a territory which under the Mexica was incorporated as a western enclave into the tribute district of Cuernavaca. Hence, turning to the Mendoza Codex we find Coatlan listed in the Cuernavaca district (f.23) which, like that of Huaxtepec (f.24v), belonged to the metropolitan area around which spread the four Mexica provinces. Corroborating this system, the boundary towns in the Coatlan Map neatly match Mexica tribute towns in the provinces, with

	Xochicalco PSP/ Palace Stone	Coatlan Map	Mendoza ff.23-4v, 36
1. Tlachco ball court			
2. Tlamacazapan priest river			
3. Atlicholoyan water fleeing			
4. Acatlicpac arrow above			
5. Xochitepec flower			
6. Huaxtepec guaje tree			

21 Toponyms on the Plumed Serpent Pyramid, Xochicalco.

Tlachco to the south (f.36, southern province), Tonatiuhco to the west (f.34, western province), and Malinalco to the north (f.35, western province).

As a guide to the Xochicalco inscriptions, the Coatlan Map first of all shows an affinity with the Palace Stone in having a common orientation, which puts south and the ball-court town Tlachco to the top of the text. In the southwestern corner both texts have a bird toponym, possibly Cacalotenango (crow fort) in the Stone; in the Map it is glossed Cuauhtliytlaquayan (eagle feed). The third toponym in the Stone apparently has the coils of a snake under a very non-ophidian head and eye: in the Cuernavaca Museum it is announced as Coatlan (from *coatl*, 'snake') clinching the link with the Map (its curious coils recall those of snakes in the Tepetlaoztoc Codex ff.20, 25v). Urcid and others, however, see mainly a turkey head and, sadly, may well be right (fig. 22).

At the same time the Coatlan Map reproduces several of the glyphs found in the Pyramid Sequence. Four, to the south and southeast and also in the Mendoza Codex (ff.36, 23), are the priest's river Tlamacazapan (Sequence 3), the fleeing water of Atlicholoyan, the raised arrow of Acatlicpac, and the flower of Xochitepec (Sequence 2). Other parallels lack this extra

corroboration but at least establish relative positions in the surrounding landscape, like the coyote river source to the west (possibly Cocoyotlan), the gesturing thin man to the southeast, and the rabbit to the east. There is a further possible parallel between the Pyramid Sequence and the Mendoza Codex (f.24v) in the guaje tree of Huaxtepec, the Mexica tribute centre to the east which lay beyond the bounds of the Coatlan Map (col. pl. 9). The presence of a sign for Huaxtepec on the Pyramid accords with details in the Náhuatl epic of Tepoztecatl, which specifically recounts how this hero liberated neighbours of eastern Tepoztlan, among which Huaxtepec is found, from the murderous tribute demands of Xochicalco.[7]

As for the structure of the Pyramid text, it is clearly significant that the hinge between Sequences 2 and 3 should be to the west, the direction with which Xochicalco identified itself, as did Tenochtitlan later, in the larger scheme of Mesoamerican history. Further, the total of the toponyms in each of the two parallel streams of Sequence 2 is sixteen; this same total governs subject towns in such sources as the Coixtlahuaca Lienzo 1 and the Tepexic Annals (final four pages, 49–52; Jansen 1992b), and through its binary logic $(16=2^4)$ recalls just the anatomical concept highlighted throughout this Sequence: human

a   *b*   *c*

22 *Versions of the glyph 'Coatlan'.*
a) Indistinct rubbing in Cuernavaca Museum catalogue; b) Lorenzo 1989; c) Urcid 1994.

teeth. The open, heavily-toothed jaw that accompanies the tribute subjects in this Sequence has been read as a sign for tribute payment, according to a discourse of feeding and sustenance consonant with the fact that the toponym Cualac, whose glyph is precisely an open jaw with teeth, derives from the term for the saliva or drool which can be life sustaining (fig. 23). Moreover, tooth (*tlantli*) coincides etymologically with the standard Náhuatl locative and place-name ending *-tlan*. In any case, the distinctive jaw glyph in Sequence 2

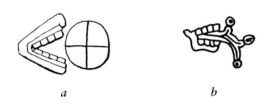

a   *b*

23 *Jaw and tooth signs.*
a) *Xochicalco; b) Cualac, Mendoza.*

points us numerically to the total of toponyms in the Sequence, indicating that, as 16+16, north and south, they may also be counted as the teeth of the upper and lower mandible.

In the arrangement of toponyms on the Xochicalco Pyramid there is, then, a firm suggestion of the importance of pattern and cipher

in statements of political and economic power, one amply testified to and developed in the codices with respect to the human body (teeth, digits, limbs, orifices of head and body), the phases of the sky, and the ritual cycles of the calendar. In Codex Mendoza itself, the subjects of the centre and the quarters are made to equal the 365 days of the year, just as the head towns in the quarters equal the 29 nights of the moon (fig. 24) and, again, just as the garrisons within and beyond the Basin equal the zodiac eleven; besides its possible relevance to the Monte Albán conquests, this last cipher determines those incised as eleven toponyms on the *cuauhxicalli* (stone offering-vessel) of Moctezuma II.[8]

Cacaxtla and Teotihuacan

Complementing these inscribed toponymic texts at Monte Albán and Xochicalco come those painted on plaster floors at Cacaxtla and Teotihuacan during the later Classic and brought to light only in the last decade. Since both these texts await publication and commentary, seminal as they are, we can here offer no more than preliminary remarks.

The Cacaxtla list of toponyms, painted on the vertical face of a small step in the floor of the Templo Rojo, runs to no more than seven items, none of which has been reliably identified with a

Gobernadores		Head towns		All towns										
Petlacalcatl	+123	centre	9	13	10	26	16	26	7	10	7	9	=	124
Atotonilco	+46	west	7	6	7	13	12	6	2	1			=	47
Tlachco	+69	south	7	10	14	12	14	8	6	6			=	70
Chalco	+82	east	7	6	22	11	11	3	22	8			=	83
Cuauhtochco	+45	north	8	7	6	7	11	7	2	5	1		=	46
	365		29											246

24 *Totals of tributary towns in the Mendoza Codex ff.19–55.*

particular place.[9] The shape of the *tepetl* sign recalls that used at Monte Albán, while its internal hatching anticipates that found in *tepetl* signs in codices from Cuextlan and Texcoco (figs 17f, m, n). The house sign in profile also matches that of the codices generally, as does the arrow of defeat. In this same Templo Rojo, there appears to be further topographic allusion in other images. The west wall prominently displays the carrying frame used by the merchants, or *pochteca*: the Náhuatl term for this object, *cacaxtli*, gives the city its current name. On the same wall large toads move up above the stairs southwards, that is in the direction of Cholula: in the *Historia tolteca-chichimeca*, or Cuauhtinchan Annals (ff.7v, 9v, 14; Kirchhoff, Güemes and García 1989), a similar toad atop a mountain serves as the emblem of Cacaxtla's neighbour and long-standing rival Cholula.

The stucco floor and certain of the walls in the newly excavated complex at La Ventilla, Teotihuacan, have an array of forty-two glyphs outlined in red; they possibly date from as early as AD 300 and yet anticipate the codices even more than the mural painting in this same city. This is especially the case with those glyphs that appeal to the iconography of the ritual cycles of the year and the *tonalamatl* (ritual calendar); several of the *tonalamatl*'s Twenty Signs are clearly legible: Snake (V), Skull (VI), Deer (VII), Water (IX), Monkey (XI), Reed (XIII), Jaguar (XIV), Movement (XVII) and Flower (XX). In general, the Teotihuacan glyphs demand to be viewed from the northern edge of the floor and read from right to left, that is from west to east. Toponymic significance has been attributed to the basket-like containers, all slightly different, in which a good many of the glyphs sit, while the determinants of these and others find ready parallels in the codex place names, for example the needle of Huitzmaloio icac (Cuauhtinchan Map 5; Reyes 1977). Especially suggestive is the row of eighteen glyphs that runs along the northern edge, framed by red lines. Certain of them find echoes in the Mendoza Codex, in the Acolhuacan tribute district that covered Teotihuacan, for example, the hummingbird place Huitzilan, and the arm of Acolhuacan itself (f.21v; fig. 25).

In structural terms, this set of eighteen suggests an interest in ritual ciphers of the kind discussed already with respect to the Xochicalco Pyramid, for eighteen is the total of the twenty-day feasts (*ilhuitl*) in the Mesoamerican year. Finding this same total of toponyms in the Guevea Lienzo, the Zapotec text from Oaxaca, Eduard Seler (1986) asserted the analogue with the eighteen *ilhuitl* of the calendar outright, in a classic study later drawn on by Marcus. In the Teotihuacan case the connection is strengthened by the fact that the eighteen toponyms are internally paired, in the fashion typical of the *ilhuitl*.

a   *b*

25 *Possible toponyms at Teotihuacan.*
a) Acolhuacan; b) Huitzilan. Left: La Ventilla; right: Mendoza f.23.

Archaeology and toponyms in the Codices

Turning now in the other direction, we may examine how toponyms in the codices may help to refine the archaeological map of Mesoamerica, providing clues to the whereabouts and nature of formerly significant centres today half-forgotten or lost to memory. A good example of how effectively codices may reveal the geographical past and the relative status of former towns is provided by the Coatlan Map, taken as a prime term of reference in the archaeological Tonatico-Pilcaya Project of the National Institute of Anthropology and History (*Instituto Nacional de Antropología e Historia* – INAH; Arana 1990). Yet much still needs to be done in the matter of reconciling what happens to have been archaeologically registered and excavated so far and the often quite different priorities indicated by native texts. For example, only sporadic attention has been given to much of the cartography defined in major bodies of texts from the Cholula Plain, the Coixtlahuaca Valley and the Upper Papaloapan, Cuextlan, and even the Basin of Mexico. The vast metropolis of Cholula is very much a case in point,[10] as is Matlatlan (Maltrata), a focus in the migration from Chicomoztoc for whole waves of Chichimecs who went on to settle in the Cholula Plain, Coixtlahuaca and the Basin.

Then, even when a site has been recognized and excavated, advantage is not always taken of the vivid detail recorded in the codices. The huge city recently 'discovered' to the northeast of the Cholula Plain, and now officially called Cantona, appears to have been well known to the authors of the codices. At least, in Cuauhtinchan Map 1, the Chichimec boundary town Tepeyahualco, with which Cantona is all but continuous, includes a highly suggestive conjoint glyph: below a lavishly attired ruler, smoking lava indicates the volcanic rock on which the latter town is unusually and exclusively built (col. pl. 10).[11] Again, Tepexic de Rodríguez, a little-explored site in the boundary area between Cholula, Coixtlahuaca and the Mixteca, is identified in a great number of texts

from those arenas, Chichimec, Mixtec, Chocho, Cuicatec, which have been largely ignored by archaeologists. Tepexic's vast walled citadels and terraces stand unquestionably as the main focus of interest, and therefore possible provenance, of the longest native annals extant, Vindobonensis obverse. In this magnificent text, the glyphs for Tepexic (split mountain), nearby Tliltepexic (chequerboard) and Huehuetlan (old man and woman) dominate the centre (raised conjoint toponym p.32) that is surrounded by its four tributary quarters (conjoint toponyms pp.35–6, 39, 43–4, 48). Firmly locating the Tepexic glyph of the codices in its former landscape is critical to a proper understanding of Chichimec settlement and, before that, of the full geographical range of the Mixtec annals (fig. 26).

By far the clearest and most dramatic case of literary pointers of this kind occurs in the first of the Xolotl Maps, which record the Chichimec ancestry of the founders of the city of Texcoco (Dibble 1980). In this text, entering the highland Basin from the north, along a route later followed by the Mexica, the Chichimec leader Xolotl and his son Nopaltzin conduct a survey of principal sites in the area (col. pl. 11). Four are shown to be of archaeological significance: Tula (Hidalgo) and a place near Tepetlaoztoc now not surely identifiable, each with only one pyramid (bottom left corner and centre right); and Teotihuacan and Cahuac, each with two pyramids (top left corner and lower centre right). All but Teotihuacan are identified as Toltec and are shown to be falling apart and grass-covered through disuse. The relative status attributed to these places is highly pertinent to the models set up by modern archaeology. That of world-famous Teotihuacan, with its two pyramids, causes less surprise than that of Tula, which today is glorified as the original home of the Toltecs. That this highland Tula in fact once had only the lesser status shown by the single small pyramid in the Xolotl Map is confirmed by Ixtlilxochitl, the Cuauhtitlan Annals (Bierhorst 1992: 28–37) and several other native sources

In texts from:
Mixteca

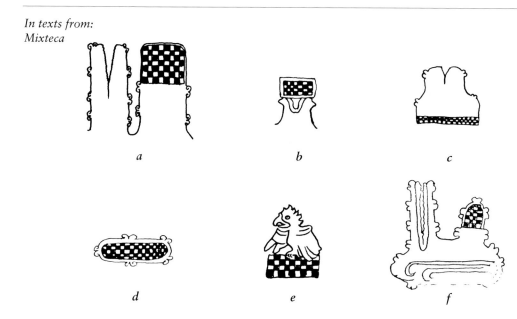

Coixtlahuaca and Upper Papaloapan

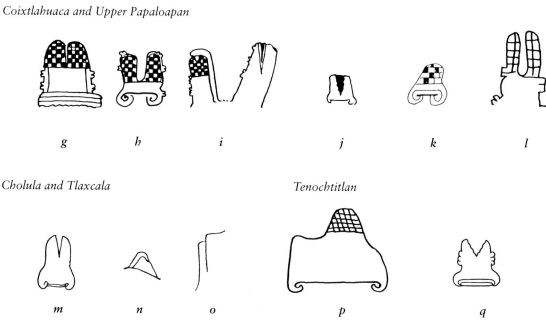

26 *Glyphs for Tepexic in texts from surrounding towns.*
a) Tepexic (Vienna p.32); b) Tilantongo (Bodley p.5); c) Nochistlan (Fragment); d) Coatepec (Lienzo);
e) Teozacoalco (Nuttall p.60); f) Tututepec (Colombino pp.3-4); g) Tequixtepec (Lienzo 1); h) Coixtlahuaca
area (Gómez de Orozco); i) Coixtlahuaca (Fonds Mexicains 20); j) Coixtlahuaca (Seler Lienzo II);
k) Tlapiltepec (Lienzo); l) Cuicatlan (P. Diaz); m) Centepetl (Heye Lienzo); n) Cuauhtinchan (Map 2);
o) Tlaxcala (Lienzo); p) Acatzinco (Dehesa p.18); q) Tenochtitlan (Mendoza f.42).

a   *b*   *c*

27 Glyphs for Cahuac.
a) Itzcuintepec Codex; b) Xolotl Map 1; c) Tochpan Lienzo 2 (phonetic, from cacao).

which note that it was founded late, not the first but the last in the long line of Toltec capitals. The biggest surprise is however Cahuac, a name now known to only a handful of specialists. According to the Xolotl Map, Cahuac with its two huge Toltec pyramids was greater than the three other sites – that is greater even than Teotihuacan, an astounding claim which finds some echo in such Cuextlan texts as the Tochpan (Tuxpan) Lienzos, and the Itzcuintepec Genealogy, where it is identified by the same upright frog glyph as in the Xolotl Map (fig. 27). Named Caguala in Spanish colonial maps and located near Ixhuatlan de Madero, Cahuac is registered as a site by INAH, though unexcavated.[12] Given the huge respect for this 'lost' metropolis shown in a range of native sources, it is pertinent to wonder what effect its exploration might have on our notions of Mesoamerican history, especially that grossly under-excavated part that concerns the Toltecs.

Having surveyed these four archaeological sites, Xolotl and Nopaltzin set up their own political strongholds at Tenayuca and then Texcoco and mark out the boundaries of their part of the Chichimecatlalli or Chichimec domain. In so doing they name places which in several cases are confirmed as common boundary marks in texts from contiguous Chichimec arenas, namely Cuextlan, Tlaxcala and the Cholula Plain, this last arena finding a common boundary in turn with Coixtlahuaca. In this, the Xolotl Maps and other codices in the Chichimec tradition establish a system whose remarkable geographical coherence has been almost entirely overlooked, along with Chichimec claims to a history that begins before, rather than after, the founding of highland Tula, and long before Xolotl. Recognizing this mass of written Chichimec evidence can only enhance our still patchy understanding of the map of Late Classic and Postclassic Mesoamerica.

Conclusion

The toponyms inscribed and painted at archaeological sites in Mesoamerica stand as an antecedent and corollary for those depicted in the codices, within what Eduard Seler called the *patrimonium commune* of the region. This is true when it comes to deciding locations on the map for specific glyphs, and in the matter of the conventional design of glyphs and the structuring of them according to ritual ciphers and patterns. At the same time, the glyphs in the codices may conversely inform attempts to interpret those found in the ancient cities. Moreover, they may serve as a valuable geographical guide to the past in general, highlighting the centres and arenas shaped by Toltec, Mixtec, Chichimec and Mexica in the successive story of empire, just as they strengthen the claims pressed by native communities today.

Notes

1. The enduring role of Techialoyan toponyms is brought out in the case of Calacoayan Book, recently brought to light in the British Library, which was presented as legal evidence in a boundary dispute as late as 1802 (Brotherston 1995a: 185–8; cf. also Galarza 1988; Wood undated). Early pictographic statements of land-ownership continue to hold the highest interest for local inhabitants, examples being the Techialoyan-owning municipios of the Estado de México anxious about the proposed new Toluca airport, as well as Tepoztlan, Morelos, currently in dispute with a Chicago-based property company.

2. On phonetics, see Nicholson 1966, Valle 1994 and Winter *et al.* 1994, which deems Zapotec writing 'non-phonetic'. On 'place' as opposed to 'emblem' glyphs of the lowland Maya, see Stuart and Houston 1994.

3. Basic studies for particular regions include those of Smith 1973; König 1984; Yoneda 1981; Barlow 1949. Macazaga 1979 offers a popular compilation.

4. The Ahuelican design is reproduced and discussed in Coe, Diehl *et al.* 1995: 234. The other two items are now housed respectively in the museum in Tepeyahualco run by Sr Limón, and in the Chimalacatepec Museum, San Juan Tlacotenco (for access I thank Gerónimo Franco; see also Broda and Maldonado 1998). The arrangment of 'teeth-bricks' in the Tlacotenco jade, three rows of seven, is exactly reproduced on Building J glyph 7). Understanding of Monte Albán script and power has now been much advanced by Marcus's subsequent work (1992) and the studies of Winter (1994), Urcid (1993, 1994) and Moser (1977 – my copy of which I owe to John Monaghan).

5. Spencer 1982; Hunt 1972; on the complex question of the Coixtlahuaca and Upper Papaloapan region and its self-image in local codices, *lienzos* and scrolls see Parmenter 1982; König 1984; Acuña 1989, 1991; Brotherston 1995a; Geist 1990. Cuicatlan is the first of four Building J toponyms examined in Marcus 1980; her 1992 study (pp.394–400) adds a further 'twenty or so', of which twelve are illustrated, though not compared with other sources or located on the map, and two, Sosola and Chilapan, are given proper names. One,

unspecified, is said also to be in Mendoza: the Chilapan in this source lies far off in Guerrero, and Sosola, though local, is an unlikely candidate, since its key element, a piercing awl, relies on Náhuatl phonetics (*tzo-*). Her 'smoke' glyph, if it is that, could possibly be Poctlan, well positioned in the Tochtepec district in Mendoza (f.48).

6. Hosler *et al.* 1990; Ixtlilxóchitl 1975–7, 1:283

7. Verazaluce MS, in González Casanova 1975; Maldonado 1990; Brotherston 1995b.

8. The 'Moctezuma' *cuauhxicalli* was recently reproduced in colour in *Arqueología Mexicana* 1, 4 (November 1993):12; on elevens, see Brotherston 1992: 66–7.

9. Minimal monochrome versions of the Cacaxtla glyphs appear in Vergara 1990: 64. For access to the Teotihuacan glyphs, I am grateful to Rubén Cabrera, who has also given a preliminary account of them (1997); I am indebted to Tony Aveni for photographs of these glyphs.

10. The most splendid of the surviving ritual screenfolds, Borgia, has often been thought to stem from Cholula. A close reading of the place elements in its Fire-Kindling chapter (pp. 48–53) confirm this is so. As the place of stairs, it lies between Yaotlan (SE), Nacapauaxqui (NE), Calpan (NW) and the 'shot-deer' place (SW); cf. Brotherston 1998.

11. Yoneda 1981: 164; this Tepeyahualco (Cantona?) glyph was chosen as cover design in Reyes 1977. On the question of Chichimec maps and arenas, see Dibble 1980; Kirchhoff, Güemes and García 1989; Parmenter 1982; for the under-acknowledged arena of Cuextlan, defined by the Tochpan Lienzos (Melgarejo Vivanco 1970) and the newly assembled Itzcuintepec texts, see Brotherston 1995a: 62–97. Byland and Pohl 1994 offer an excellent account of local Mixtec geopolitics, but are less convincing in their interpretation of texts that deal with wider empire, saliently Fonds Mexicains 20 (Coixtlahuaca Map) and Vindobonensis (Tepexic Annals); see also Caso 1977–9; Jansen 1992a, 1992b; Stokes 1995; Brotherston 1985.

12. Caguala appears in the seventeenth-century map *Nova Hispania et Nova Galicia*; cf. also Melgarejo Vivanco 1970; Brotherston 1995a: 96.

References

Acuña, René (1982–8) *Relaciones geográficas del siglo XVI,* 10 vols. México: UNAM.

Acuña, René (1989) *Códice Baranda.* México: Toledo.

Acuña, René (1991) *Códice Fernández.* Leal, México: UNAM.

Arana, Raul Martín (1990) *Proyecto Coatlan. Area Tonatico-Pilcaya.* México: INAH.

Barlow, Robert (1949) *The Extent of the Empire of the Culhua Mexica.* Berkeley: University of California Press.

Berdan, Frances and Patricia Rieff Anawalt (1992) *Codex Mendoza.* Berkeley: University of California Press.

Bierhorst, John (1992) *History and Mythology of the Aztecs. The Codex Chimalpopoca.* Tucson: University of Arizona Press.

Bradomín, Jose María (1992) *Toponimia de Oaxaca (Crítica etimológica).*Oaxaca: no publisher (3rd edn).

Broda, Johanna and Druzo Maldonado (1998) 'Culto en la cueva de Chimalacatepec, San Juan Tlacotenco, Morelos', *Graniceros, los que trabajan con el tiempo. Cosmovisión y meteorología indígenas de Mesoamérica,* Beatriz Albores and Johanna Broda (eds). Toluca: Colegio Mexiquense.

Brotherston, Gordon (1985) 'The Sign Tepexic in its textual landscape', *Iberoamerikanisches Archiv* 11, 209–51.

Brotherston, Gordon (1992) *Book of the Fourth World. Reading the Native Americas through their Literature.* Cambridge: Cambridge University Press.

Brotherston, Gordon (1995a) *Painted Books from Mexico. Codices in the United Kingdom Collections and the World They Represent.* London: British Museum Press.

Brotherston, Gordon (1995b) 'Las cuatro vidas de Tepoztecatl', *Estudios de Cultura Náhuatl* 25, 185–205.

Brotherston, Gordon (1998) 'Reading ancient landscapes in and through the codices', *Indiana Journal of Hispanic Literatures* 13: 98–109.

Byland, Bruce and John Pohl (1994) *In the Realm of 8 Deer. The Archaeology of the Mixtec Codices.* Norman: University of Oklahoma Press.

Cabrera Castro, Rubén (1997) 'Glifos teotihuacanos sobre un piso de estuco', *II Simposio Códices y documentos sobre México,* Vol. 1, 393–406. México: INAH.

Caso, Alfonso (1964) *Interpretación del Códice Selden.* México: Sociedad Mexicana de Antropología.

Caso, Alfonso (1965) 'Zapotec writing and calendar', *HMAI* 3, 931–47.

Caso, Alfonso (1977–9) *Reyes y reinos de la Mixteca,* 2 vols. México: FCE.

Coe, Michael D., Richard A. Diehl, David A. Freidel, Peter T. Furst, Kent Reilly III, Linda Schele, Carolyn E. Tate, Karl A. Taube (1995) *The Olmec World: Ritual and Rulership.* Princeton: Princeton University Press.

Dibble, Charles E. (1980) *Codice Xolotl,* 2 vols. México: UNAM.

Diehl, Richard A. and Janet Catherine Berlo (1989) *Mesoamerica after the Decline of Teotihuacan AD700–900.* Washington DC: Dumbarton Oaks.

Galarza, Joaquín (1988) *Estudios de Escritura Indígena Tradicional Azteca-Náhuatl.* México: Archivo General de la Nación.

Geist, Ingrid (1990) 'Reflexiones Acerca de las Prácticas Rituales en San Andrés, Teotilalpan'. Tesis profesional. México: ENAH.

Glass, John B. (1964) *Catalogo de la colección de códices.* México: Museo Nacional de Antropologiá.

González Casanova, Pablo (1977) *Estudios de Lingüística y Filología Nahuas.* México: UNAM.

Hirth, Kenneth (1989) 'Militarism and social organization at Xochicalco', *Mesoamerica After the Decline of Teotihuacan AD 700–900,* Diehl and Berlo (eds), 69–81. Washington DC: Dumbarton Oaks.

Hosler, Dorothy, Heather Lechtman and Olaf Holm (1990) *Axe-Monies and their Relatives.* Washington DC: Dumbarton Oaks.

Hunt, Eva. (1972) 'Irrigation and the socio-political organization of the Cuicatec cacicazgos', *The Prehistory of the Tehuacan Valley* 4, F. Johnson and R. MacNeish (eds), 162–261. Austin: University of Texas Press.

Ixtlilxóchitl, Fernando de Alva (1975–7) *Obras Históricas,* Edmundo O'Gorman (ed.). México: UNAM.

Jansen, Maarten (1992a) *Crónica Mixteca (Zouche-Nuttall).* México: FCE.

Jansen, Maarten (1992b) *Origen e Historia de los Reyes Mixtecos (Vienna).* México: FCE.

Kirchhoff, Paul, Lina Odena Güemes and Luis Reyes

García (1989) *Historia Tolteca-Chichimeca*. México: FCE.

König, Viola (1984) 'Der Lienzo Seler II und seine Stellung innerhalb der Coixtlahuaca Gruppe', *Baessler Archiv* 32, 229–320.

Lorenzo, Antonio (1989) *Historia de Xochicalco: por sus pinturas y esculturas*. México: Porrúa.

Macazaga Ordoño, César (1979) *Nombres Geográficos de México*. México: Innovación.

Maldonado Jiménez, Druzo (1990) *Cuauhnahuac y Huaxtepec: Tlalhuicas y Xochicmilcas en el Morelos prehispánico*. México: UNAM.

Marcus, Joyce (1980) 'Zapotec writing', *Scientific American*, February, 50–64.

Marcus, Joyce (1992) *Mesoamerican Writing Systems. Propaganda, Myth, and History in Four Ancient Civilizations*. Princeton: Princeton University Press.

Melgarejo Vivanco, José Luis (1970) *Códices de Tierras. Los Lienzos de Tuxpan*. México: Petróleos Mexicanos.

Morante, Rubén (1993) 'Evidencias del conocimiento astronómico en Xochicalco'. Tesis de Maestría. México: ENAH.

Moser, Christopher L. (1977) *Ñuiñe Writing and Iconography of the Mixteca Baja* (Publications in Anthropology, no.19). Nashville: Vanderbilt University.

Nicholson, H.B. (1966) 'Phoneticism in the late Pre-Hispanic Central Mexican writing system', *Mesoamerican Writing Systems*, E. Benson (ed.), 1–46. Washington DC: Dumbarton Oaks.

Parmenter, Ross (1982) *Four Lienzos of the Coixtla-huaca Valley*. Washington DC: Dumbarton Oaks.

Quiñones Keber, Eloise (1995) *Codex Telleriano-Remensis*. Austin: University of Texas Press.

Reyes García, Luis (1977) *Cuauhtinchan vom 12. bis zum 16. Jahrhundert*. Wiesbaden: Franz Steiner.

Seler, Eduard (1904a) 'Die Ruinen von Xochicalco', *Gesammelte Abhandlungen*, Berlin, 2, 128–67.

Seler, Eduard (1904b) 'Die Ausgrabungen am Orte des Haupttempels in Mexiko', *Gesammelte Abhandlungen*, Berlin, 2, 767–904.

Seler, Eduard (1986) *Plano jeroglífico de Santiago Guevea* (1905). México: Ediciones Guchachi' Reza.

Smith, Mary Elizabeth (1973) *Picture Writing from Ancient Southern México. Mixtec Place Signs and Maps*. Norman: University of Oklahoma Press.

Spencer, Charles S. (1982) *The Cuicatlan Cañada and Monte Albán: A study of primary state formation*. New York: Academic Press.

Stokes, Philip (1994) 'The Origin of the Mixtec Lords as Told in Their Own Histories'. Ph.D. Dissertation. Colchester: University of Essex.

Stresser-Péan, Guy (1995) *El Códice de Xicotepec*. México: FCE.

Stuart, David and Stephen Houston (1994) *Classic Maya Place Names*. Washington DC: Dumbarton Oaks.

Urcid, Javier (1993) 'The Pacific Coast of Oaxaca and Guerrero. The westernmost extent of Zapotec script', *Ancient Mesoamerica* 4, 141–65.

Urcid, Javier (1994) 'Monte Albán y la escritura zapoteca', *Escritura Zapoteca Prehispánica. Nuevas Aportaciones*, Marcus Winter (ed.), 77–96.

Valle, Perla (1994) *Códice Tepetlaoztoc (Códice Kingsborough)*. Toluca: Colegio Mexiquense.

Vergara Berdejo, Sergio de la L., Andrés Santana Sandoval *et al.* (1990) *Cacaxtla. Proyecto de Investigación y Conservación*. Tlaxcala: Conaculta/INAH.

Winter, Marcus, ed. (1994) *Escritura Zapoteca Prehispánica. Nuevas Aportaciones*. Oaxaca: INAH

Wood, Stephanie (undated) 'Prose and Cons: The Historicity of Títulos and Techialoyan Codices'. Unpublished manuscript.

Yoneda, Keiko (1981) *Los Mapas de Cuauhtinchan y la historia cartográfica prehispánica*. México: Archivo General de la Nación.

4. The Indigenous Past in the Mexican Present

John Gledhill

This paper discusses Mexico's indigenous peoples, the descendants of the people who created and used the artefacts displayed in the Mexican Gallery at the British Museum. This is a delicate matter: indigenous Mexicans are perfectly capable of speaking for themselves and are pursuing active struggles to achieve greater respect from the rest of Mexican society and a fairer share of the nation's resources. I will outline some of the main issues in the campaign for a new deal for indigenous peoples later on, and my objective in this paper is simply to offer some thoughts on why it is so important that we listen attentively to their voices and recognize their present as well as past achievements. To this end, I will offer a brief survey of the five hundred years of history which have elapsed since the Spanish conquest, highlighting the ways in which indigenous peoples have always been actors in that history.

Colonialism, nation-states and the remaking of indigenous societies

Modern Mexico is a nation-state built on European colonial foundations. Part of the prehispanic culture area archaeologists define as 'Mesoamerica' is not in modern Mexico, but in Guatemala, Belize, El Salvador and the other Central American countries. Not only did prehispanic societies and cultures form regionally distinct traditions – even though they interacted with each other, and, in the case of western Mexico, with South American cultures – but Spanish colonialism and its aftermath reorganized their structures and boundaries in profound ways. This reorganization increased the existing regional diversity.

We can look at the impact of colonialism in general terms or focus on how it was different in different areas. As far as the general picture is concerned, the Spaniards redefined all indigenous peoples as a particular caste of colonial society, as 'Indians' rather than Nahuas, Otomis, Zapotecs and so on. Indians were obliged to pay tribute to the Spanish King, and they became wards of the colonial state and the Church. The Spaniards came to the New World in search of gold and silver, but stayed to exploit their new colonies and their peoples in a multitude of other ways, ranging from forced labour and tribute to the more indirect systems of exploitation associated with forced deliveries or purchases of commodities (*repartimientos de mercancías*) (Gledhill 1988).

We should also remember that some Spaniards came to conquer new worlds for the Christian God, and that they could be equally brutal in their means for achieving that end. There were more enlightened voices among the European conquerors, such as Father Bartolomé de las Casas. Yet even the contemporary critics of the Spanish colonial regime shared certain ideas of European superiority with their less enlightened fellows, as they strove to create Christian utopias in this New World that had been won for Christ. The first dimension of Spanish reorganization of indigenous society was, then, an intentional, bureaucratic, top-down one. It aimed to give indigenous people a new identity as an ethnic underclass in a colonial society. But there was a second, unintentional dimension: over the century which followed the Conquest, the populations of the new colonial indigenous communities were decimated by the import of Old World diseases.

In the colonial period indigenous peoples throughout Mesoamerica were forced to change their ways of living. They often had to change their patterns of settlement, they became tribute-payers to the Spanish Crown, and they became subject to the authority of the Catholic Church. The process of social and cultural change under the Spanish was not, however, simply a matter of European imposition. It was also a matter of indigenous responses to new circumstances which were creative and active, rather than passive. They involved both resistance and accommodation, and often a degree of both at the same time. So it was not just the Spanish who remade indigenous societies – they remade themselves and, in doing so, had a significant influence on the evolving colonial culture of the European immigrants and people who came to see themselves as of mixed race, the *mestizos*.

This remaking of indigenous society has been a continuous process up to the present day. But it is a process which is heavily influenced by the different kinds of interactions which take place between indigenous groups and other elements of regional societies. The nature of the colonial experience was significantly different for the indigenous communities of central Mexico and the Maya of the Yucatan, for example (Farriss 1983). It was different again for the Maya who lived in Chiapas (Wasserstrom 1983; García de León 1985). Differences in the colonial transformation of indigenous society have had a profound impact on the place of indigenous people in modern national societies.

The differences seem apparent if we compare the recent histories of Mexico and Guatemala.[1] In 1992 the Salinas de Gortari administration in Mexico modified Article Four of the National Constitution, to recognize the country for the first time as a multicultural society. Although the special rights that were extended to indigenous peoples in Mexico still fall far short of the provisions of UN Agreement 169 and the demands made by the hemispheric indigenous rights movement, further progress on indigenous rights issues in Mexico seemed possible after they became central to the negotiations between the government and the Zapatista Army of National Liberation (EZLN) in San Andrés Larráinzar, Chiapas. It was Mexico which received the flood of Maya refugees from the Western Highlands of Guatemala who were displaced by the genocidal campaign of the Guatemalan military. Few people would deny that it was better to be a Maya on the Mexican side of the international border during this period, but how much better is a more difficult question. As a preliminary answer, I will simply cite the words of Manuel Camacho Solís, the first negotiator appointed by the government to talk to the Zapatista rebels: 'On behalf of all the Mexicans, I wish to ask the pardon of the indigenous peoples of Chiapas.'

It is true that the rebellion in Chiapas reflected a specific regional history and the specific conditions which emerged in the Lacandón forest sub-region during the 1970s and 1980s,[2] but it would not be true to say that indigenous grievances are restricted to Chiapas. Other regions of Mexico a long way from Chiapas have erupted in indigenous peasant protest in the not very distant past. An important example is the Huasteca Potosina in the mid-1970s, which led to the last major episode of land reform in Mexico (Schryer 1990). The Zapatista uprising of January 1994 became a focal symbol for an upsurge of indigenous peasant activism in an arc of territory extending up through Oaxaca to Veracruz, and sympathy for the movement's aims is evident in other rural areas beyond that zone (fig. 28).

If one looks at the social statistics, it is clear enough that apologies are, indeed, in order: indigenous communities display worse figures than other parts of Mexican society on every index of health, nutrition and education, and indigenous people are also much more likely to find themselves unjustly imprisoned and tortured by the police (Amnesty International 1995). Arbitrary gaoling is a routine tactic of the local political

28 *Emiliano Zapata, the revolutionary agrarian leader from the state of Morelos who was murdered in 1919, remains a living symbol for popular movements throughout Mexico.* (Photo: John Gledhill)

bosses, or *caciques*, who still dominate rural communities in regions like Chiapas, but indigenous people who have offended nobody remain vulnerable to judicial arbitrariness throughout the country, particularly if they do not speak Spanish. It is therefore clear that the present president of Mexico, Dr Ernesto Zedillo Ponce de León, was correct to emphasize the urgent need for reform of the justice system in his 1994 election campaign, and that indigenous people deserve the highest priority in measures to ensure that all Mexicans enjoy the civic and human rights which they are guaranteed by the constitution. What the recent changes to that constitution guarantee to indigenous people as distinct from other Mexican citizens are, however, *cultural* rights – rights to have their 'difference' from other Mexicans respected – and these rights are thus far seen officially as rights that *indígenas* should claim as *individuals*. The negotiations in San Andrés

Larráinzar were, however, focused on more sweeping demands. One was that indigenous communities be allowed to exercise collective, communal rights over all the resources in their territories – including, for example, forest and mineral resources which have previously been exploited by outsiders or the state itself. Another was that indigenous communities should receive constitutional guarantees of their right to exercise autonomy in the management of their internal affairs. 'Autonomy' means that they should, for example, be able to elect their political representatives by consensus in communal assemblies rather than on the basis of individual votes in a ballot box, and that indigenous territories should be recognized as political units within the national territory.[3]

This much broader programme of indigenous demands, shared by indigenous groups in many parts of Mexico, throws into focus a number of important questions about the present and future place of indigenous peoples in Mexican national society. The most important one from the point of view of gaining an historical understanding of what is specific to the Mexican context is: why, exactly, are Mexico's Indians officially defined as an 'ethnic minority' within a society in which the identity of the majority is defined as *mestizo*?

The specificity of Mexico
One of the principal factors which distinguishes Mexico from other Latin American countries which have large indigenous populations is the way indigenous people were incorporated into colonial society, although developments after national independence are also very important (Mallon 1992, 1995). Central Mexico *was* the centre of Mesoamerica in the demographic sense. In the old heartlands of the Mexica empire, Spaniards and Indians interacted socially on a day-to-day basis to a much greater extent than in most other regions of Latin America. Indian villages continued to exist, with their own lands and specific local identities (Lockhart 1992). But most villagers also worked on the lands of the Spanish and *criollo*[4] landowners as seasonal labourers at harvest time, and much of the pre-colonial indigenous élite moved into the Spanish sector of colonial society. Through a lengthy process which the Mexican anthropologist Guillermo Bonfil (1990) called 'de-Indianization', the central region of Mexico became a society of *mestizos* in the cultural rather than biological sense. A majority of the people came to see themselves primarily as 'peasants', and eventually as Mexicans, rather than as Nahuas, Otomis or members of one of the other ethnic groups which had inhabited the central valley before the arrival of Cortés.

This tendency for what became Mexico to develop a *mestizo* core was reinforced by the economic development of the region to the north of Mexico City known as the Bajío. In the pre-colonial period the Bajío had been sparsely populated by nomadic 'Chichimecs'. These

original indigenous inhabitants of the countryside were then driven up into the remote sierras by the incoming settlers. Many of the new settlers were also people of indigenous stock, but from central and western Mexico. The indigenous migrants who settled in the Bajío lost their separate identity and merged into the rest of the population of *mestizo* peons, tenant farmers and urban artisans. In 1810 the once relatively prosperous working population of this economically dynamic region rose up under the banner of Father Hidalgo, not simply to fight for independence from Spain but to secure redress for class grievances in what could be seen as the first attempt to make a popular social revolution on Mexican soil (Tutino 1986).

As the nineteenth century progressed, agrarian grievances became important in many other areas. After liberal governments decreed the disentailment of communal land in the second half of the century, these agrarian conflicts increasingly involved indigenous communities which had previously been relatively pacific. Community lands were taken over by landed estates (*haciendas*) or in some cases by indigenous village bosses allied to *mestizo* outsiders (col. pl. 12). These transformations of class structures made the subsistence of poorer families increasingly precarious. But the peculiarities of Mexican history were reinforcing a cultural divide between the north and the centre and the deep south as far as popular social movements were concerned.

De-Indianization of the centre strengthened the peasant or *campesino* identity at the expense of ethnic identity, and popular nationalism was strengthened by the military interventions of the United States and the French (Knight 1992). The struggles between Liberals and Conservatives during the nineteenth century expressed an increasingly important opposition between the old colonial centre and its élite on the one hand, and provincial élites and urban middle-class groups on the other. This helped to make liberalism a popular cause rather than simply an élite ideology, giving Mexican liberalism a radical, Jacobin tendency which found its fullest expression in the Mexican revolution of 1910 against the dictator Porfirio Díaz.

Indians were by no means marginal to these social and political upheavals. Yet, on the surface at least, they tended to participate as agrarian rebels and supporters of a broader popular political agenda. Some fought alongside *mestizo* or 'white' *ranchero* rebels whose main concern was with defending their autonomous regional power against political centralizers in Mexico City (Knight 1986). Others, like the original Zapatistas in the state of Morelos, demanded not only land, but municipal autonomy and reform of the justice system (Warman 1988), demands that belonged to a wider popular liberal tradition. They did not generally emphasize a demand for recognition as indigenous people. Nevertheless, as Florencia Mallon (1995) has demonstrated, there is a more complex hidden history to be uncovered here. The indigenous communities of the Northern Sierra of Puebla state, which allied with the liberal factions in the civil wars of the nineteenth century, for example, did so on the basis of their own interpretations of the liberal land laws, rejecting the idea of converting communal village landholdings into individual private plots which could be sold. This brought them into violent conflict with the government when their former liberal allies sought to impose a model of 'modernization' as private property relations guaranteed by a strong central government under the restored republic. Despite repression, persistent commitment to their own agenda led these communities to ally with Porfirio Díaz, when, as a rebel against the liberal regime, he spoke for peasant land claims and municipal autonomy. Intransigent not only in their defence of their lands but also in their rejection of a national state which denigrated their indigenous identities in racist discourses of social control that sought to transform them from dangerous 'others' into individualized 'citizens', they were again at the forefront of the national revolt

against the much transformed Porfirio Díaz of 1910.

Race played a central role in colonial and post-colonial ideologies. As far as the *criollo* 'white' élite of post-independence Mexico was concerned, any uprising involving indigenous people was a 'caste war'. Social status in colonial society was measured, as it was in Reconquest Spain, by purity of blood, and it was a society constructed on the principle that Indians were a different and inferior race. The Indians were placed under the tutelage of the Church, and their tributes were to fill the coffers of the Spanish Crown. To be an Indian was therefore to live in one of the Indian communities recognized as a legal and administrative unit by the colonial government. To belong to the 'Republic of Indians' was to be a member of a nation within a nation, as well as a member of a lower ethnic caste in a hierarchic order. Indian blood was, however, redeemable as far as colonial ideology was concerned: by 'whitening themselves', the descendants of Indians could theoretically pass into the upper, European-derived, sector of society (Lomnitz-Adler 1992)

Here I should stress that I am talking about ideology. Actual practice was much more flexible than this ideology suggests, and this has prompted some historians to argue that colonial Mexico was not really a caste society at all, but one held together by patron–client relations. This is certainly the kind of model which best describes the relations between indigenous people and the white cattle-rancher political bosses of the Huasteca, for example, at least prior to the 1960s: the rancher bosses spoke indigenous languages and communicated with their indigenous clients in a tone which was hierarchic, paternalistic and authoritarian, but also expressed a certain respect for the Indians' dignity (Schryer 1990; Lomnitz-Adler 1992). People who were born in indigenous communities could, in practice, 'pass' into the non-Indian sector by going to live elsewhere, speaking Spanish, and changing their style of dress. De-Indianization or 'mestizoization' was a result of this social and cultural strategy rather than of biological 'race mixing'.

Whether people pursued the strategy or not depended on regional circumstances. Wasserstrom (1983) suggests that most people in central Chiapas chose not to 'pass' into the lowest social stratum of *mestizo* (or, to use the local term, *ladino*) society, because this offered them no material or social status advantage. The Bajío, on the other hand, illustrates the opposite tendency: most people 'passed'. But the overall effect of all the processes I have described was to make the Mexican nation a society with a *mestizo* majority, in which 'Indians' appeared to have become a minority, concentrated in the periphery rather than the centre of the modern nation-state (Bonfil 1990).

To some extent, this peripheralization was also a reflection of indigenous tactics: some indigenous people had moved into the remote sierras to seek refuge from colonial forms of oppression, as Aguirre Beltrán (1970) argued. Others were driven into such marginal areas by the expanding military frontier of colonization, as in the Bajío. The fundamental basis of the division was, however, the 'de-Indianization' of the colonial heartland and the less intense kind of Spanish–Indian interaction which characterized much of the 'deep south'.

Being 'indigenous' today is not, therefore, a question of people's genes. It is a question of the defence of indigenous social identities over centuries of struggle – some of it violent, but much of it non-violent, everyday struggle – to conserve a distinctive culture and to prevent outsiders from robbing the people of their remaining land and social dignity.

Indigenous culture in a regional context

To illustrate this point more concretely, I will take the example of the state of Michoacán in which I have done most of my own ethnographic work. The core indigenous population of Michoacán today remains quite visible, distinguishing itself by items of dress, housing, artisan production and ceremonial life (col. pl. 13). Indigenous communities co-exist with *mestizo* peasant communities and with communities which see themselves as 'white' people of European descent, *rancheros*. Distinctions of skin colour and other ideas about 'race' are still very central to social attitudes in everyday life in Michoacán, but the point I want to stress is that 'ethnic' distinctions are more malleable than one might imagine, because they are built on *social* distinctions. What actually happened historically in this region is extremely complex: there was a considerable amount of population shift and redefinition of community identities and boundaries. Both some of the indigenous communities and some of the *mestizo* communities have a long history of struggles over land, but what has happened in more recent years is a growth of a kind of 'ethnic politics' that did not exist before.

As a matter of historical fact, the indigenous inhabitants of the region in pre-colonial times did not belong to a single 'ethnic' group or speak the same language. Some were Náhuatl speakers, like the Mexica, and others were Purhépecha speakers, members of the ethnic group which built the Tarascan empire which halted Aztec expansion into western Mexico and humiliated the Aztec army on the battlefield.[5] This fact is salient to contemporary ethnic politics, since people now think of themselves as Purhépecha and build their identity around the idea that they are 'not Aztecs'. Aztec identity has become associated with Mexico City's politico-bureaucratic domination, and with an unfair distribution of national resources between the capital and the provinces.

The Purhépecha ethnic leaders are mostly local professionals,[6] and what they want is for their culture to be respected in its own right. They demand that its conservation and revival be given resources commensurate with its importance. In this case, then, the indigenous past is being reactivated and re-evaluated to contend with a changing present. Nor is this simply a matter of the strategies of intellectual leaderships. We can also find poor people who have invaded land on the edges of towns re-evaluating their 'Indianness' in reflecting on the economic rights they are claiming. People who once saw themselves as *mestizos* may remember that a grandparent spoke Purhépecha and decide to re-identify themselves with that part of their heritage. One of Michoacán's most important contemporary independent rural social movements, the Unión de Comuneros 'Emiliano Zapata', has been successful at recruiting both *mestizos* and indigenous people, by encouraging the former to abandon their prejudices and re-identify themselves with their indigenous side (fig. 29 and col. pls 14–16).

This is very significant. Modern Mexican nationalist ideology was built around an attempt to valorize *mestizaje*. After independence, the *criollo* élite maintained the ideological model of caste distinctions inherited from the colonial social order. That order was, however, challenged by rising politicians which the élite classified as *mestizos*, who identified with liberalism. Benito Juárez, the hero of Mexican national liberation from the French, was, in fact, of Zapotec Indian ancestry, although he had proved a ruthless repressor of Indian resistance to the disentailment of communal land when he was governor of his native Oaxaca, and was equally ruthless in his efforts to repress his former allies in the indigenous communities of the Northern Sierra of Puebla once they had helped him back to national power, as I noted earlier. Despite his Indian origins, Juárez became an archetypical representative of what we could term a 'mestizo authoritarianism'. This is what underpinned the emergence of what is perhaps confusingly called an *indigenista* ideology in post-revolutionary Mexico (Becker 1987; Mallon 1992).

Official indigenismo and indigenous culture

After the 1910 revolution, the official *indigenista* position was an assimilationist one: Indians should be able to benefit from the revolution in terms of material progress, and get special treatment in

29 *Decorating the streets in memory of the dead, Patamban, Michoacán.* (Photo: John Gledhill)

terms of agrarian reform and public education, but the aim was to bring them into the cultural mainstream of a Mexico which was defined as a *mestizo* culture in a particular way. What was special about Mexican culture was its creative blending of the indigenous and the European. Mexicans were heirs to both these great cultural traditions, the fusion of which represented something new, special and positive. This view of Mexicanness emphasizes the achievements of (dead) Mesoamerican civilization, but it is in danger of downgrading Mesoamericans who lived outside that tradition of urban civilization. It also downgrades living Indians and the whole history of indigenous post-colonial cultural development in favour of an emphasis on *mestizaje* as a progressive historical process. It identifies social progress with 'whitening' and discourages Mexicans from identifying with their indigenous side against the models of economic and social 'modernization' associated with European and northern capitalist societies (individualism, consumerism, technological mastery of the environment and so on).

There are perfectly good reasons for wanting to celebrate the fusion of European and indigenous culture in Mexican history, as Carlos Fuentes suggested in his BBC television series *The Buried Mirror* (Fuentes 1992). There are also good reasons for wanting to explore the ways that the culture of indigenous communities in the colonial period incorporated European ideas and elements of European popular culture. But there are less good reasons to justify an obliteration of the continuing and future contributions of indigenous communities to national life. The cultural interchange went both ways, and the dominant *mestizo* local cultures owe more to indigenous society than culinary styles and a great many loan words. *Mestizo* folk-Catholic religion, for example, is just as permeated with indigenous elements as Indian religion is permeated with popular practices derived from Europe. There are good reasons for rejecting the argument that indigenous people themselves only feigned conversion to Catholicism and continued to secretly worship their old gods: Christianity had a fundamental impact on the 'deep structures' of indigenous religious belief and practice (Ingham 1986; Brading 1990). Yet what emerged was a distinctively Mexican Christianity and a set of religious institutions and practices which indigenous people could often reclaim as their own even when they were not, strictly speaking, prehispanic indigenous customs which were simply continued under colonial conditions. In the case of the Maya, the indigenous version of Christian cosmology, which fused indigenous ideas of cyclical time (*ka'tuns*) with Franciscan apocalyptic millenarianism, eventually became a counter-hegemonic ideology looking towards the day when the Spanish would be driven out (Brading 1990).

Most of Mexico's so-called 'caste wars' in fact had more modest objectives, and it is mainly in the south rather than in central Mexico that indigenous movements which sought the overthrow of Spanish rule are found. But throughout the colonial period, indigenous communities everywhere had devised strategies for marking and defending their social boundaries and resources. Indigenous people have also devised ways of managing their interactions with other social groups which rescue their own dignity by subverting the claims to superiority of others without appearing to challenge them. One way of describing the relationship between resistance and accommodation in indigenous Mexico is to say that indigenous people in Mexico developed a kind of 'double consciousness'. They can use different communicational codes when dealing with outsiders than those they use amongst themselves. They have learned when it is pragmatically desirable to talk the official language of the state and use the law, without necessarily accepting the ultimate validity of official categories and criteria of justice. The pressures towards assimilation have been strong, but they have been counteracted by one simple fact: the promise of material progress and social equality made by post-revolutionary *indigenismo* was not honoured.

Cultural continuity, transformation and reconstruction

This lack of material progress is one of the reasons for the creation of new forms of ethnic politics in Mexico. Regional social movements concerned with land and jobs in marginalized areas have found celebrating ethnic identity a useful way of bringing people together and giving them dignity. Changes at the international level have helped fuse

30 *Mestizo beneficiaries of land reform (ejidatarios) parade with the national flag. The official ideology of the post-revolutionary state envisaged an assimilation of indigenous peoples into a mestizo nation. (Photo: John Gledhill)*

environmental concerns with those of indigenous rights and fostered the development of indigenous identities which cross national boundaries. This is a major development, because until recently many indigenous identities were strictly local, confined to villages rather than regions and ethnic groups. As I pointed out earlier, some kinds of indigenous movements have emphasized the goal of cultural revindication without pursuing more traditional kinds of agrarian demands. Today's panorama is extremely complex, and marked by various opposing tendencies: we have movements which stress particular ethnic identities rather than a pan-Indian identity; we have movements which emphasize specific identities within major indigenous groups, like the Maya, and others which seek to foster a general indigenous identity; and we have indigenous movements which seek to pursue specific ethnic demands in the context of a broader popular struggle which centres on alliances between different social and ethnic groups.[7] Some of Mexico's indigenous movements enjoy very cordial relations with the government; others belong to the more radical sectors of the opposition (fig. 30).

All this suggests that indigenous identity politics today are closely bound up with the politics of the modern state. They are also bound up with processes of cultural globalization through which local movements learn about what is happening elsewhere in the world. Today, quite uneducated people in rural areas use words like 'ecology' and objectify their cultural traditions. Many of the current perspectives of indigenous cultural politics in Mexico reflect the way local 'organic intellectuals' are linked into wider international networks of communication and diffusion of ideas. Indigenous leaders in other countries have often criticized Mexican movements for being contaminated by the popular non-Indian agrarian revolutionary tradition, and for having failed in the past to be 'ethnic' enough. This criticism often turns on the idea that indigenous peoples see land as more than an economic resource, and should ideally view it as community 'territory' in the sense of cosmically bounded space. Today we do find this more 'indigenous' perspective being emphasized, which no doubt in part reflects this wider context. Nevertheless, important though global information flows and the influence of a transnational discourse of 'rights' and associated legal frameworks have become, they are still subject to the same kind of varying local interpretations as ideas emanating from élite groups in the last century. Nor do I seek to give the impression that it is impossible to identify genuine cultural continuities from the prehispanic past in contemporary indigenous practices or that everything about contemporary indigenous politics should be explained in terms of intellectual leaderships and diffusion of foreign models.

First, the very fact that indigenous culture has been a peasant culture through most of post-Conquest history makes it plausible to argue that local communities would preserve heterodox cultural practices and their own local traditions, whatever efforts were made to impose the ideas of dominant social groups on them from above. It is quite common, for example, to find that both indigenous and *mestizo* communities maintain local models of place and space in which ancient sites are still seen as significant elements of the cultural landscape. To some extent, at least, this landscape remains cosmic, meaningful, and subject to forces which do not belong to the world of secular rationalism. Secondly, there are other 'ethnogenetic' processes at work today which can give rise to a collective rediscovery or reinvention of indigenous identity without an initial lead from intellectual leaderships.

A good example of the latter is provided by the Mixteca Alta region of Oaxaca (Kearney 1986, 1991). This was an area where interaction between Indians and non-Indians was particularly limited during the colonial period and the nineteenth century. Indian communities placed more stress on local, communal identities than any overarching Mixtec ethnic identity, and conflicts between

villages were much more significant than conflicts between Indians and non-Indians. What changed the Mixteca was the increasing inability of the people to subsist on increasingly eroded land.

As a socially marginalized group, they first sought a solution to their problems by migrating to work as labourers on the large capitalist farms in northern Mexico. There they suffered from every conceivable kind of abuse and deplorable living and working conditions, but the experience sharpened their sense of collective identity and equipped them for the next step, which was undocumented migration across the border into the United States. Today, the Mixtecs are a highly self-conscious population, and their experience of discrimination and deracination is what has forged this new ethnic consciousness. They have organized themselves to rebuild their home communities and to fight for better conditions in the United States more effectively than many other groups who have suffered less. They exemplify two important principles: first, the ability of ordinary people to reconstruct their own ways of life, and second, the role that ethnic identity may come to play in that reconstruction. What is important here is that the Mixtec migrants were people who had been downgraded and stigmatized in two societies: they reacted to that situation by using their specific ethnic identity as a way of reasserting their dignity and value as human beings (in the face of the failure of the 'civic' model of identity to work for them).

Contemporary Mixtec ethnic identity is 'new' in historical terms, but I have argued that Mexico's indigenous people have, in fact, been continuously reinventing themselves since the Conquest, often in ways that are relatively invisible. To members of the dominant social groups, Indian villagers in Mexico often appeared both acculturated and submissive. Underlying this outward appearance, however, were what James Scott (1990) has termed 'hidden transcripts' of resistance. The deferential behaviour and few words in Náhuatl quite often masked an ironic and scarcely respectful response to authority. As I have stressed, in some parts of Mexico Indian communities were not subjected to strong interference by the colonial regime until late in the colonial period. The first major revolts in much of the Maya area outside Chiapas were concerned with outside interference in community religious organization and the introduction of a more rapacious and less tolerant secular clergy, not with land grabbing. Qualitative differences in the experience of colonialism had an impact on the extent to which prehispanic cultural practices were conserved, and on the way these fused with European elements. But it does not really repay us to look at the culture of contemporary indigenous people simply as a question of 'survivals'[8] any more than it is valid to define indigenous people in terms of inheritance of genes.

Christianity and other aspects of European culture have played a significant part in the evolution of post-Conquest indigenous cultures, and there are some areas of culture, such as gender relations and notions of sexuality, where I think it is important to recognize significant breaks between pre-colonial and post-colonial culture throughout Mexico.[9] But even institutions which Europeans sought to impose on the indigenous peoples, such as the *cofradías* or religious brotherhoods, were taken over, turned to indigenous ends, given indigenous meanings and used by Indian communities to defend their own boundaries (Gruzinski 1990). In today's ethnic politics we often recognize elements of 'invented tradition', but this is only a problem for people who think that the proper state of cultural traditions is to be dead.

What is unacceptable about the official Mexican national myth is the way it peripheralizes the living Indian culture and perpetuates a notion of social progress as 'whitening oneself'. Under contemporary conditions, a variety of forces are opening up possibilities for a radical reappraisal of the indigenous side of Mexican identity, but we should not underestimate the barriers which remain embedded in the legacy of past social and

political history. Practices of discrimination remain integral to the daily social life of many regions, and indigenous militancy can still evoke reactions redolent of the old fears of 'caste war', as evidenced by the reaction of many city-dwellers, particularly in the north, to the Chiapas uprising. As Héctor Díaz-Polanco (1992) has pointed out, Latin American élites have manipulated ethnic distinctions to their own advantage, and the fact that 'ethnicity' is reproduced through practices of domination can influence the ways in which indigenous people resist their oppression. After six months of violence in which nine of their number had been assassinated and a twelve-year-old boy had an ear slashed off by the wife of a leading *mestizo* politician, the Mixtec inhabitants of the municipality of Tlacoachistlahuaca, Guerrero, demanded a separate *municipio*, although they constitute 60 per cent of the population of the current, *mestizo*-dominated municipality (*La Jornada*, 25 November 1995). Persistent and acute oppression may thus eventually convince people that separatism is the only way out, and some indigenous organizations are taking an increasingly separatist position, arguing that 'Indians' are essentially 'different' from other people in a way which might be seen as a kind of inversion of the racist ideas of dominant *criollo* and *mestizo* élites (Hale 1994). Current demands for indigenous 'autonomy' do not, however, necessarily entail a rejection of the rights and responsibilities of national citizenship. What happens in the future will depend crucially on the reactions of the wider society to the increasingly articulate voices of 'deep Mexico'.

Valuing indigenous people for what they are

We should celebrate the opening of the Mexican gallery of the British Museum as a blow against a view of universal history which sees Western civilization as the end of human social evolution, and shackles the rise of urban civilization to Eurocentric theories of historical progress. We should not, however, assume that the indigenous contribution to Mesoamerican culture history ended with the Conquest, nor should we folklorize contemporary indigenous people.

Fortunately, they will not let us do that. We live in an age where 'culture' of every conceivable sort is commoditized, and where 'cultural difference' is being reasserted by a number of forces, including tourism. Indigenous artisans are as interested as anyone else in making a living, and tourists can be attracted by all manner of experiences, including ecological devastation and peasant insurrections. Middle class Mexicans continue to be shocked by the conditions in which many of their indigenous countrymen live in rural villages and these problems still need to be taken more seriously by government. Yet the last five hundred years of Mexican history show us quite clearly that indigenous people are not just victims but actors.

I can underscore this conclusion by offering another example of how some of the less visible members of Mexico's indigenous population live with the contradictions of their situation in the modern world.[10] The Río Balsas region of Guerrero is a relatively marginalized zone occupied by Náhuatl speakers. Life in the home villages is hard because the soils are eroded and artisan production is not so much an income supplement as a necessity in a complex struggle to make ends meet. The villagers make masks, which are exported to the United States by an American woman to satisfy the tastes of the California market for exotica. Even this does not allow them to stay put in their *ranchos*, however, and they have sallied forth to cut cane in other states like Colima and Michoacán. In this context, we might see them simply as downtrodden, racially stigmatized, migrant farm workers living in the insanitary quarters provided for them in the villages around the sugar mills illustrated in the photographs. But there is more to this picture than meets the eye (figs 31–2 and col. pls 17–18).

31–2 *Migrant cane cutters from Náhuatl-speaking communities in Guerrero state, photographed in the housing provided for them in the village of Los Limones, Michoacán. The 'galleries' had earth floors, and the families slept on the straw mats seen rolled up in the background.* (Photos: Kathy Powell)

The older generation did not speak Spanish as a first language, but the younger people, and especially the younger women, are not so readily distinguishable in terms of cultural markers as 'Indians' unless they choose to be so distinguished. The earnings of cane-cutters are very poor, but they are sufficient to pay a bus fare to Tijuana, the point of departure for an undocumented trip over the US border. This is one way forward through the stream of history that leads to the future, if not an entirely unproblematic one, given falling real wages and growing anti-immigrant sentiment 'on the other side'.

But the Río Balsas contains other surprises. It was decided, as so often happens, that this marginal area would be a good place to build a new hydro-electric dam to serve the distant Mexico City–Toluca conurbation. Since the dams silt up rapidly, even constant levels of demand for electricity create problems. The project would, of course, displace the Nahuas, who turned out to be rather more numerous than the government and World Bank had thought them to be. They also turned out to be far more capable of organizing

themselves than anyone had expected. They blockaded major traffic arteries outside their home region and mounted a mass media publicity campaign against the project. After that, the Nahuas of the Río Balsas ceased to be a forgotten people and were negotiating with Dr Arturo Warman, one of Mexico's most distinguished anthropologists, at that time head of the National Indigenous Institute.

In the course of the discussions, one of their spokesmen observed that indigenous people in Guerrero deserved greater respect from the rest of the nation, and drew the government negotiators' attention to the existence of important archaeological monuments of the Olmec period in the region. The indigenous past thus erupted again into the Mexican present. The force of the indigenous rhetoric did not lie in the existence of any direct cultural link between the formative peoples of Guerrero and the contemporary Nahuas. It lay in the fact that contemporary indigenous peoples are capable of demanding dignity and respect for what they are as well as for what they were.

Notes

1. On Guatemala, see for example Smith (ed.) (1990) and Wilson (1991).
2. For the longer-term historical background see, for example, Wasserstrom (1983), García de León (1985), Rus (1983, 1994). For more recent developments affecting the indigenous population of Chiapas in general, see, for example, Cancian (1992) and Collier (1994a). For the analyses of the specific causes and context of the EZLN rebellion, see Harvey (1994), Collier (1994b), and Leyva Solano and Ascencio Franco (1996). Tello Díaz (1995) offers an analysis of the rebellion from a position closer to that of the Mexican government.
3. For a fuller discussion of how these demands, along with others including the rights of women, became integral to the Zapatista movement, see Stephen (1995).
4. Persons of European descent born in the colonies, as distinct from *peninsulares* born in Spain.
5. Purhépecha is a unique language, which does not belong to one of the four main language families into which the different Mesoamerican tongues can be classified. Náhuatl was the most widely spoken language. For the most recent scholarship on prehispanic Michoacán, see Boehm de Lameiras (coordinator) (1994).
6. On the contemporary reconstruction of Purhépecha culture, see Zárate Hernández (1994).
7. For comparative perspectives, see, for example, Wilson (1993), Hale (1994) and Watanabe (1995).
8. The problem with the argument of Guillermo Bonfil to which I referred earlier is that his notion of a 'deep Mexico', which persists despite 'de-Indianization' and the 'modernization' of

Mexican society, is a largely romantic construct which focuses on the 'survival' of a timeless Indian culture, reduced to a list of elements or traits.

9. It is, however, also true that contemporary communities exhibit differences with regard to questions of gender roles: in Michoacán women from indigenous communities are much more likely to perform heavy manual work in agriculture, which *mestizo* males regard as socially demeaning for females. Male obsessions with containing women within the domestic sphere and guarding their 'purity' (as a means of defending male honour) are not, however, restricted to *ranchero* or *mestizo* communities, a problem which has been highlighted by the EZLN's marrying of indigenous and women's rights (Stephen 1995: 90–91).

10. The discussion of the situation of the migrants in Michoacán which follows has benefited from the research of Kathy Powell, who also took the photographs. I am indebted to Jane Hindley for information on the movement against the dam project in the Río Balsas.

References

Aguirre Beltrán, Gonzalo (1970) *Regiones de Refugio.* México, D.F.: Instituto Indigenista Interamericano.

Amnesty International (1995) *Mexico. Human Rights Violations in Mexico: A Challenge for the Nineties.* AI Index: AMR 41/21/95. London: Amnesty International.

Becker, Marjorie (1987) 'Black and white and color: The search for a Campesino ideology', *Comparative Studies in Society and History*, 29, 453–65.

Boehm de Lameiras, Brigitte (coordinator) (1994) *El Michoacán Antiguo: Estado y Sociedad Tarascos en la Época Prehispánica.* Zamora: El Colegio de Michoacán and Gobierno del Estado de Michoacán.

Bonfil Batalla, Guillermo (1990) *México Profundo: Una Civilización Negada.* México: Editorial Grijalbo.

Brading, David (1990) 'Images and prophets: Indian religion and the Spanish Conquest', *The Indian Corporate Community of Colonial Mexico: Fifteen Essays on Land Tenure, Corporate Organization, Ideology and Village Politics*, Arij Ouweneel and Simon Miller (eds). Amsterdam: CEDLA.

Cancian, Frank (1992) *The Decline of Community in Zinacantán: Economy, Public Life, and Social Stratification 1960–1987.* Stanford: Stanford University Press.

Collier, George A. (1994) 'The new politics of exclusion: Antecedents to the rebellion in Mexico', *Dialectical Anthropology* 19(1), 1–43.

Collier, George A. (1994b) *Basta! Land and the Zapatista Rebellion in Chiapas.* Oakland: Food First Books.

Díaz-Polanco, Héctor (1992) 'Indian communities and the quincentenary', *Latin American Perspectives* 19(3), 6–24.

Farriss, Nancy M. (1983) 'Indians in colonial Yucatan: three perspectives,' *Spaniards and Indians in Southeastern Mesoamerica: Essays on the History of Ethnic Relations*, Murdo J. MacLeod and Robert Wasserstrom (eds), 1–39. Lincoln: University of Nebraska Press.

García de León, Antonio (1985) *Resistencia y Utopía*, vol.1. México: Ediciones Era.

Gledhill, John (1988) 'Legacies of empire: Political centralization and class formation in the Hispanic-American world', *State and Society: The Emergence and Development of Social Hierarchy and Political Centralization*, John Gledhill, Barbara Bender and Mogens T. Larsen (eds), 302–19. London: Routledge.

Gruzinski, Serge (1990) 'Indian confraternities, brotherhoods and *mayordomías* in central New Spain. A list of questions for the historian and anthropologist', *The Indian Community of Colonial Mexico: Fifteen Essays on Land Tenure, Corporate Organizations, Ideology and Village Politics*, Arij Ouweneel and Simon Miller (eds), 205–23. Amsterdam: CEDLA.

Hale, Charles (1994) 'Between Che Guevara and the Pachamama: Mestizos, Indians and identity politics in the anti-quincentenary campaign', *Critique of Anthropology* 14(1), 9–39.

Harvey, Neil (1994) 'Rebellion in Chiapas: Rural reforms, Campesino radicalism and the limits to *Salinismo*', *Rebellion in Chiapas*, Neil Harvey with Luis Hernández Navarro and Jeffrey W. Rubin

(Transformation of Rural Mexico Series, No. 5), 1–43. La Jolla: University of California, San Diego, Center for US-Mexican Studies.

Ingham, John M. (1986) *Mary, Michael and Lucifer: Folk Catholicism in Central Mexico.* Austin: University of Texas Press.

Kearney, Michael (1986) 'Integration of the Mixteca and the western US-Mexico region via migratory wage labor', *Regional Impacts of U.S.-Mexican Relations,* Ina Resenthal-Urey (ed.) (Monographs Series, No. 16.), 71–102. La Jolla: University of California, San Diego, Center for US-Mexican Studies.

Kearney, Michael (1991) 'Borders and boundaries of state and self at the end of Empire', *Journal of Historical Sociology* 4(1), 52–74.

Knight, Alan (1986) *The Mexican Revolution. Volume I: Porfirians, Liberals and Peasants.* Cambridge: Cambridge University Press.

Knight, Alan (1992) 'The peculiarities of Mexican history: Mexico compared to Latin America, 1821–1992', *Journal of Latin American Studies,* 24, Quincentenary Supplement, 99–144.

Leyva Solano, Xóchitl and Gabriel Ascencio Franco (1996) *Lacandonia al filo del Agua.* México: Fondo de la Cultura Económica.

Lockhart, James (1992) *The Nahuas After the Conquest: A Social and Cultural History of the Indians of Central Mexico: Sixteenth through Eighteenth Centuries.* Stanford: Stanford University Press.

Lomnitz-Adler, Claudio (1992) *Exits from the Labyrinth: Culture and Ideology in the Mexican National Space.* Berkeley: University of California Press.

Mallon, Florencia E. (1992) 'Indian communities, political cultures and the state in Latin America', *Journal of Latin American Studies* 24, Quincentenary Supplement, 35–53.

Mallon, Florencia E. (1995) *Peasant and Nation: The Making of Postcolonial Mexico and Peru.* Berkeley, Los Angeles and London: University of California Press.

Rus, Jan (1983) 'Whose Caste War? Indians, Ladinos and the Chiapas "Caste War" of 1869', *Spaniards and Indians in Southeastern Mesoamerica: Essays on the History of Ethnic Relations,* Murdo J. MacLeod and Robert Wasserstrom (eds), 127–69. Lincoln: University of Nebraska Press.

Rus, Jan (1994) 'The "Comunidad Revolucionaria Institucional": The Subversion of Native Government in Highland Chiapas 1936–1968', *Everyday Forms of State Formation: Revolution and the Negotiation of Rule in Modern Mexico,* Gilbert M. Joseph and Daniel Nugent (eds), 265–300. Durham and London: Duke University Press.

Schryer, Frans J. (1990) *Ethnicity and Class Conflict in Rural Mexico.* Princeton: Princeton University Press.

Scott, James C. (1990) *Domination and the Arts of Resistance: Hidden Transcripts.* New Haven: Yale University Press.

Smith, Carol A. (ed.) (1990) *Guatemalan Indians and the State, 1540–1988.* Austin: University of Texas Press.

Stephen, Lynn (1995) 'The Zapatista Army of National Liberation and the National Democratic Convention', *Latin American Perspectives* 22(4), 88–99.

Tello Díaz, Carlos (1995) *La Rebelión de las Cañadas.* Mexico: Cal y Arena.

Tutino, John M. (1986) *From Insurrection to Revolution in Mexico: Social Bases of Agrarian Violence, 1750–1940.* Princeton: Princeton University Press.

Warman, Arturo (1988) 'The political project of Zapatismo', *Riot, Rebellion and Revolution: Rural Social Conflict in Mexico,* Friedrich Katz (ed.), 322–37. Austin: University of Texas Press.

Wasserstrom, Robert (1983) *Class and Society in Central Chiapas.* Berkeley: University of California Press.

Watanabe, John M. (1995) 'Unimagining the Maya: Anthropologists, others, and the inescapable hubris of authorship', *Bulletin of Latin American Research* 14(1), 25–45.

Wilson, Richard (1991) 'Machine guns and mountain spirits: The cultural effects of state repression among the Q'eqchi' of Guatemala', *Critique of Anthropology* 11(1), 33–61.

Wilson, Richard (1993) 'Anchored communities: Identity and history of the Maya-Q'eqchi' *Man* 28(1), 121–38.

Zárate Hernández, José Eduardo (1994) 'La fiesta del Año Nuevo Purhépecha como ritual político. Notas en torno al discurso de los profesionales indígenas purhépechas', *El Verbo Oficial: Política Moderna en Dos Campos Periféricos del Estado Mexicano,* Andrew Roth Seneff and José Lameiras (eds), 99–124. Zamora: El Colegio de Michoacán and Universidad ITESO.

5. Ritual and Economy of the Preclassic Maya: Recent Evidence from Cuello, Belize

Norman Hammond

The origins of Classic Maya civilization in the tropical lowlands of Central America have in the past two decades been the subject of intensive investigation by numerous projects. The British Museum's Corozal Project of 1973–8 was the first to pursue a research agenda explicitly aimed at resolving the problem of Maya cultural origins in the Preclassic period before AD 300, as well as the first to adopt a regional rather than single-site based approach, in its survey of northern Belize and its excavations at Nohmul, Colhá, Santa Rita Corozal, San Esteban and finally Cuello. It was, however, soon joined by teams working at many other Preclassic sites in both Belize and Guatemala: the decade 1975–85 saw more emphasis on Preclassic problems than on most other aspects of Maya archaeology. Investigations at Komchén, Edzná, Nakbé, El Mirador, Tikal, Lamanai, Cerros, and other Late Preclassic sites of the central and northern Maya lowlands documented the emergence of a complex society in the latter part of the first millennium BC, manifested in large-scale architecture, elaborate architectural sculpture, and an iconography that suggests a coherent controlling ideology. The control of human and material resources evidenced by the massive ceremonial precincts and landscape manipulation of the largest sites showed a society on the brink of civilization.

The cultural tradition thus established continued unbroken for nearly 1,500 years and has been the focus of scholarly attention for more than a century and a half; but the prior development of the first farming communities,

before the evolution of such proto-urban centres, still needs further study and is still yielding surprising new data. Here I will outline some of the evidence for Preclassic Maya culture over the period from around 1200 BC to AD 200 which we have recently encountered at Cuello in northern Belize (fig. 33), a small community, probably never of great importance in the Maya world of its day, which has, however, yielded useful evidence on the economy, technology, architecture, burials and ritual of the early Maya.

Cuellos

The site lies about 5 kilometres west of Orange Walk Town and on the crest of the low ridge between the Río Hondo and Río Nuevo at some 20 metres elevation. This has an undulating microtopography resulting from solution and drainage patterns, and the visible structures of the ancient Maya settlement lie on the elevated areas. They include a minor ceremonial precinct of two plazas, each with a pyramid c. 9 metres high and a number of long 'range-type' structures. Around and south of this precinct is a zone of dispersed settlement covering about 1.6 square kilometres. As initially mapped, it comprised some 200 platforms and structures; the discovery of ground-level dwellings, invisible on the surface and detectable only by excavation, led Wilk and Wilhite (1991) to suggest a population of 300–400 in the Early Middle Preclassic prior to 600 BC, rising to 2,200–2,600 in the Late Preclassic and a peak of 3,400 in the Early Classic period ending c. AD 600. Further mapping in 1992 added another

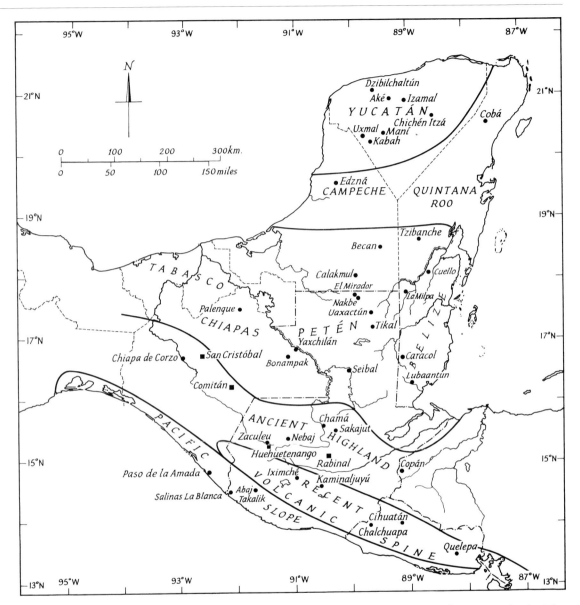

33 *Map of the Maya Area, showing major environmental zones, some important prehispanic and colonial sites, and the location of Cuello in northern Belize.*

fifty-two structures, and a population increase of 25 per cent over the published estimates would not be unreasonable, to around 500 in the Early Middle Preclassic and perhaps 3,000 in the Late Preclassic.

The Classic period ceremonial precinct lies close to the northern limit of settlement, but Platform 34 (some 300 metres to the south and the apparent core of the Preclassic community) consisted of a centrally located platform, an isolated flat elevation with a small superimposed pyramid, Structure 35, at its western end. This area has been the major locus of excavation (see Hammond 1991; Hammond *et al.* 1991, 1992, 1995). This paper introduces further analyses of some pre-1990 material as well as summarizing more recent results.

Excavations between 1975 and 1980 and again from 1987 to 1993 yielded a cultural sequence beginning in the terminal Early or Early Middle Preclassic, *c.* 1200 BC in calendar years and ending in the Postclassic *c.* AD 1000–1250. The ceramic chronology begins with the Swasey complex, which is followed by the Bladen, both within the Swasey ceramic sphere (Kosakowsky 1987). The Bladen complex and the coeval Bolay complex at neighbouring Colhá have links with the Xe sphere of the Pasión basin, the Eb complex at Tikal, and more distantly with the Xox complex of the Salama valley in Baja Verapaz (Sharer and Sedat 1987). These suggest a span of *c.* 900–650 BC for Bladen, and a date of perhaps 1200–900 BC for Swasey (Andrews and Hammond 1990; Housley, Hammond and Law 1991; Law, Housley, Hammond and Hedges 1991). The sequence continues after 650 BC with the Late Middle Preclassic López Mamom and Late Preclassic Cocos Chicanel complexes, full members of their respective ceramic spheres, with a Mamom-Chicanel transition generally placed at about 400–300 BC.

On Platform 34 an area of *c.* 3,000 square metres was stripped to the latest surviving construction phase (XIII) of Late Preclassic date *c.* AD 250, revealing poorly preserved structures on the north and south sides of the platform top and a *plazuela* group of three buildings around an enclosed patio off the northern edge of the platform, forming a late extension of it. The final Early Classic and later phase (XIV) of Structure 35 was removed except for its southwest quadrant, exposing the Late Preclassic Structure 350 buried within it. In addition, an axial trench in which earlier buildings (Structures 351–5) were recorded was sunk through Structure 35 to bedrock.

The main excavation into Platform 34 was an area 30 metres by 10 metres (the 'main trench') just east of Structure 35, dug in stages between 1976 and 1993 (col. pl. 19). Platform 34 proved to be of Late Preclassic construction, built *c.* 400–300 BC over a courtyard group with a history going back to *c.* 1000–900 BC, and overlying still earlier buildings lacking the courtyard plan. In addition, a southern trench was dug between 1990 and 1993, linking the main trench to the south margin of Platform 34 and providing a continuous north–south section 47 metres long and up to 4 metres deep.

Buildings

Two main periods of architectural development can be defined, prior to and succeeding the transformation which took place at the beginning of the Late Preclassic period, *c.* 400 BC. The first spanned stratigraphic phases I-IVA, following an initial phase 0 when timber-framed buildings with trodden earth floors were built on the old land surface. In phase I were two very low plaster-surfaced floors less than 0.1 metres high, with eroded margins and hence irregular plan. From phase II onwards the layout consisted of low platforms tightly clustered around a patio less than 20 metres across, with the boundaries of the patio shifting no more than 2 metres in any direction over the entire period of half a millennium. The patio was surfaced by successive Patio Floors I-V and these developments are dated by pottery of the Swasey, Bladen and López Mamom ceramic complexes.

The second period, dating entirely to Cocos times, consisted of the construction and successive periods (stratigraphic phases VA-XIII) of expansion and refurbishment of Platform 34, a broad elevation with an open plaza on top and buildings on its north, south and west sides, the latter eventually becoming a 6-metre-high pyramid. The plaza was 25 per cent larger from north to south in phase VA than the phase IVA patio, and expanded even further southwards from phase VI onwards. A summary of the sequence and overall phase plans can be found in Hammond and Gerhardt (1990) and Hammond (1991: 23–60, 98–117).

It would seem that the early buildings were wholly or predominantly domestic in function and that the ceremonial architecture of the second period evolved out of a household tradition. Implicit in this is the inference that the patio group was the domain of an extended family, and that its structures and space were the loci of domestic activity. From the beginning of López Mamom, the growth in exterior space with the enlargement of the patio and the later plaza corresponds with a trend away from a solely domestic function, towards an increasing ceremonial role. By the end of phase IVA the deposition of valedictory caches in structures and in the patio indicate increased ritual activity, followed by the massive architectural transformation of phase V, the transition between these long periods of development.

This architectural transformation involved partial demolition of the buildings around the patio, infill of the patio, and the laying of thick fills over the whole courtyard group to support the first surface of Platform 34 (Plaza Floor I), accompanied by offerings ranging from a cache of jade beads to the slaughter and mass burial of thirty-two individuals (col. pl. 20). The transition could have been triggered by a number of events, including the death of a leading personage: the presence of bone tubes carved with the woven-mat *pop* motif (which in Classic Maya iconography designates rulership), of possible ancestor bundles of excarnate bones, and of numerous sacrificial victims in the accompanying mass burial would be consonant with such an explanation.

The initial phases of Platform 34 had no discernible ceremonial structures; the first such was the second stage of Structure 352, with its axial burial, followed by the third stage with a dedicatory cache including a stingray spine, an object used in bloodletting and linked to ancestor veneration. The west side of the plaza thus became occupied by a succession of ceremonial structures. On the north the subcircular buildings seem to have been domestic in function, their pattern of burials of all ages and both sexes consistent with

this, and the marking off of private space around them suggesting public use of the plaza in front, presumably in connection with the use of the shrine on the west side. Ceremonial use of the plaza included erection of the stela and the deposition of offerings, including dedicatory caches of pottery vessels in the floor fill, two caches of deer mandibles and a second mass burial of a dozen men. Finally, Structure 302 was erected in the centre of the plaza, associated with the existing stela, and with a burial later placed in front of its west end. The occurrence of these activities above the locus of the phase V mass burial may not be coincidental, and may further support the notion of an atavistic cult.

The excavation of Platform 34 has shown how a residential patio group grew into an élite compound with its own ceremonial precinct. The large rectangular platforms and caches at the end of the Early Period indicate changes in status, as does the human and material investment in the raising of Platform 34 at the beginning of the Late Period. Jade, *Spondylus* shells, and other imports reflect the increased access to exotic goods of the occupants of the final patio group and subsequent plaza buildings.

The first Early Period buildings were not arranged (so far as can be seen in the limited area excavated) around a patio and may have held single nuclear families if they were domestic in function; but from phase II onwards the familiar *plazuela* layout characteristic of later Maya prehistory, and generally accepted as the residence of an extended family, was present. If the view of Collier (1975) is correct – that extended families protect scarce resources, especially land, by ensuring transmission from one generation to the next, thus avoiding fragmentation – this suggests greater pressure on agricultural resources in the Maya lowlands by the early first millennium BC than archaeological evidence so far indicates. Cliff's (1988: 222) assessment that 'extended family households apparently developed from, but did not replace, a nuclear family household base' is more in accord with Wilk and Wilhite's (1991) analysis of the Cuello settlement area: that the rich had larger households (reflected archaeologically in more prominent groups of house-platforms), one of which was subsequently aggrandized into a cult focus when Platform 34 was built. While insufficient excavation has been done in the surrounding settlement area for us to be dogmatic, from phase III onwards the size of the dwellings under Platform 34 exceeds that of any other known Preclassic constructions at Cuello. This suggests that social ranking, as expressed by size of residence, may have existed from *c.* 800 BC onwards. This is corroborated by burial evidence.

Burials

A total of 162 Preclassic individuals were excavated at Cuello, 58 from the Early Period (5 Swasey, 22 Bladen, 31 López Mamom phase) of 1200–400 BC; and 104 dating to the Late Period (Cocos Chicanel phase) of 400 BC–AD 250, comprising the largest present sample of Preclassic lowland Maya burials. Most of the Early Period interments were in graves cut into house-platform floors during initial construction, during use and at abandonment, indicative of family-type residential burials as Haviland (1985) demonstrated for small Classic period residential groups at Tikal. The earliest burials of the Swasey Phase were not associated with plaster-floored houses, but their clustering suggest that they may have been dug through the earthen floor of a building at ground level. Extended supine burial (nine examples) is most common before 650 BC, but flexed, seated and disarticulated skeletons are also found; the earliest Swasey interments were oriented northwards, included both flexed and extended positions and lacked grave goods. Tightly flexed burials, still lacking grave goods, continued later in Swasey times, and deposition of pottery vessels with burials began in the Bladen phase after 900 BC. The presence of abundant grave goods, including valued exotics such as jade and marine shell (col. pl. 21) in children's graves

suggests that status was already ascribed on the basis of descent, as well as by achievement in adult life. A shift from a slight majority of females over males among sexable adults (7:10) before 650 BC, to a marked preponderance of males (16:3) in 650–400 BC foreshadows the male domination of public burial in this locus in later centuries. Burial 22, into the centre of the patio floor around 650 BC, is the first plausible evidence of public veneration of a lineage ancestor, although Robin (personal communication) suggests that the anomalous burials in the western buildings of the patio group in Bladen times can also be regarded as designated ancestors (cf. McAnany 1995).

The Bladen funerary assemblage is among the most diversified at Cuello, including pottery; a ceramic bird whistle; jade, greenstone and shell jewellery; bone and chert tools; and ground stone. The presence of jade and greenstone in burials by the end of Bladen, *c.* 650 BC, indicates the procurement of long-distance trade items for sumptuary use from as far as 350 kilometres away in the Guatemalan highlands. Two jade objects, associated with the adult female Burial 114 and the child Burial 166 are of particular interest. One is a blue jade spangle pendant (Hammond 1991: Figure 9.8n), the other a blue jade mirror-skeuomorph, or 'clamshell' pendant (fig. 34 and col. pl. 22) similar to those from Chacsinkín, Yucatan, published by Andrews (1986, 1987). The geological source for this blue jade is unknown but, as the former piece resembles blue jade spangle pendants from La Venta, it is possible that it originated as an artefact in the Gulf Coast/Isthmus of Tehuantepec region some 600 kilometres to the west of Cuello.

Although López Mamom grave goods were less varied, with pottery vessels and shell-bead jewellery being the standard offering, there was greater differentiation between individuals with and those without grave goods than in the Swasey/Bladen sample: 70 per cent of López burials had at least three offerings, the majority with three to five items. Richer burials with a high

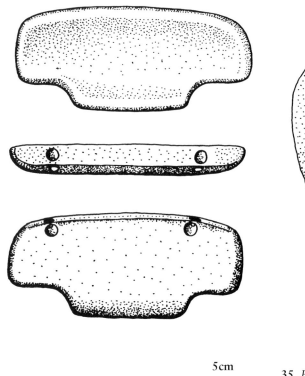

5cm

5cm

35 Bone gorget, made from a disc of human skull, from Burial 160 of c. 500–450 BC.

34 Blue jade pendant of possible Olmec origin, c. 600 BC. The rear-edge perforations conceal the suspension holes and avoid intrusion on the front face.

number of grave goods were associated with long-distance trade items; one of the most elaborate, the probably male mature adult Burial 160, had jade beads, a perforated shell, a turtle carapace (drum?), four carved bone tubes at the waist, and a bone gorget, one of the earliest known pieces of Preclassic Maya art in a coherent style and assured technique (fig. 35 and col. pl. 23). Three of the tubes bore a criss-cross design (Hammond, Clarke and Estrada Belli 1992: Figure 6) apparently attempting the *pop* woven-mat design more expertly executed on the (larger) tubes from Mass Burial 1 a half-century or so later (Hammond 1991: Figures 8.35–6). Since the *pop* motif was in Classic Maya times a symbol of regal authority, the

individual in Burial 160 may have been of importance in the Cuello community of c. 500–450 BC. The burial itself, axially placed in the building at the south end of the patio (and perhaps forming with the less well-equipped Burial 170 a double interment with a [?] sacrificed retainer), suggests a transition from venerated ancestor to a ruler with his regalia.

As noted above, access to both multiple grave goods and long-distance trade items cuts across age and sex boundaries. If generalizations on social structure could be based on so few individuals, the distribution of grave goods in the Swasey/Bladen phase would suggest some social differentiation not based on age or sex. Such a development may be related to the establishment of regional exchange networks: the presence at Cuello from at least Bladen times onwards of obsidian, from the San Martín Jilotepeque (Río

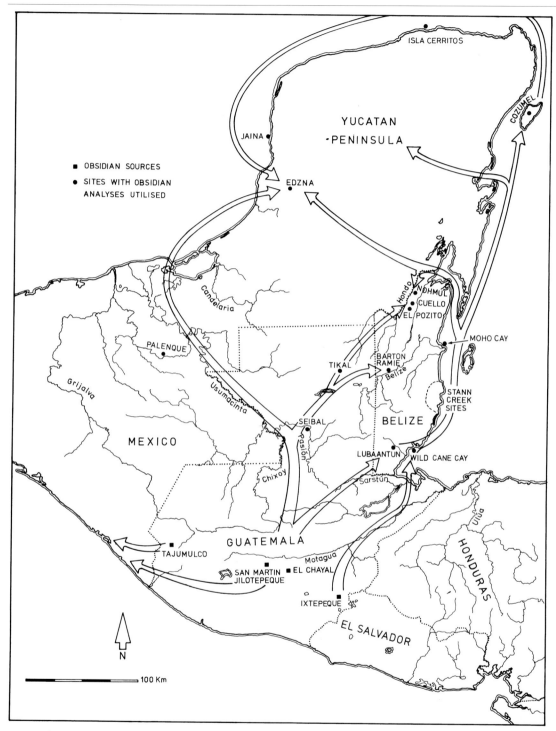

36 *Obsidian trade routes in the Maya Area, showing supply from three major highland sources to the lowlands. Preclassic Cuello received obsidian from the San Martín Jilotepeque source initially, and later from El Chayal and Ixtepeque also. Other sites with analysed obsidian samples are also shown.*

Pixcaya) source west of Guatemala City (fig. 36), and of jade jewellery in late Bladen graves, indicates that commerce was already developed. The procurement at an even earlier date of *manos* and *metates* from the Maya Mountains, 150 kilometres to the south, shows that the long-distance exchange networks that by 700 BC reached south to the Motagua Valley jade sources and further up into the volcanic highlands to the obsidian flows were extensions of existing networks, not innovations. Which of these factors were causes and which consequences remains unknown, but this development at Cuello of domestic and public architecture, and of social division exhibited in mortuary ritual, must be seen against the background of a lowland Maya society moving rapidly towards complexity in the Early Middle Preclassic period.

The largest number of burials (103 individuals comprising 68 per cent of the total Cuello sample) date to the Late Period after 400 BC. The large size of the sample and an excavation strategy exploring all Cocos Chicanel phase contexts on Platform 34 suggest that this percentage is representative of the population buried there in this period, itself perhaps drawn from the élite segment. Two mass burials account for forty-four individuals, and six other interments are associated with the rituals of platform construction and dedication attending Mass Burial 1. Thus half the sample comes from non-standard sepulture. Males were selected for public burial, implying their importance in public activity (including sacrifice) in the Cocos phase. Within the residential sector the ratio of men to women to children suggests the same family-type burial grouping seen in the Middle Preclassic patio residences; juveniles were about one-third of the buried population in both northern platforms. The ratio of adults to children is 47:0 in the public plaza area; in residential platforms the ratios are 16:10 and 31:11 respectively. Although both sexes and all age groups from infancy to old age are represented in the Cocos phase sample, it is clear that the 4.8:1 ratio of men to women does not represent a normal population distribution, and continues the male predominance noted for López times.

As in the Early Period, the mortuary pottery did not differ from that used for domestic purposes, although burials often included rather large examples of common vessel forms (unsurprising given their function of covering the body). There were a few categories of offerings unique to burials in the Cocos phase, including the single imported vessel found at Cuello (an Olocuitla Orange Usulutan bowl from El Salvador or eastern highland Guatemala), an amphora-shaped jar, and seven carved bone tubes which could have functioned as handles for feather fans or bloodletting implements.

Throughout the initial construction, use, reflooring, remodelling and eventual abandonment or destruction of a building, burials were incorporated into its structural fills and floors, indicating opportunistic sepulture in residential contexts. The association of caches with construction shows that reflooring and remodelling Platform 34 was not just a practical affair, but one accompanied by ceremony and offerings. Most consisted of or included flaring-side bowls, which when paired are set lip-to-lip, mainly of Sierra Red and Society Hall Red, the two dominant ceramic types of the Late Period. They form three main groups, all associated with construction work: dedicatory offerings for successive plaza floors on top of Platform 34; dedicatory and valedictory offerings for successive buildings on the north side of the plaza; and dedicatory offerings for successive raisings of the buildings on the west side of the Platform 34 plaza, culminating in the Early Classic pyramid, Structure 35. The number of caches is low early in the Late Period, rising to a maximum with the construction of the first pyramid on the west side of the plaza, with the erection of Stela 1, and with the deposition of Mass Burial 2. This suggests that a significant increase in the ritual status of the plaza took place around AD 100, and was maintained for some three centuries thereafter.

Economy

The development of Cuello as a community, exemplified in the architectural growth of the central locus, was underpinned by a complex and efficient subsistence economy. The traditional historic Maya diet was based on maize, beans and squash, with a small proportion of other crops, gathered foods, and animal protein; it had been generally assumed that the prehispanic economy was similar, both in its low-pressure land utilization and in the relative importance of dietary components. There was, however, little empirical evidence until the late 1970s. Although animal bones had been collected unsystematically on most Maya excavations, together with some carbonized vegetal matter and impressions on clay (e.g. Willey *et al.* 1965: 523–9), techniques of sieving for small and fragmentary bones and flotation for plant remains were introduced for the first time at Cuello. Improved excavation methods showed that the scarcity of the remains, assumed because of the tropical wet climate (Willey *et al.*: 528), was more apparent than real.

The institution of systematic recovery techniques at Cuello similar to those long used elsewhere in the world led to the recovery of abundant environmental and economic data (Hammond and Miksicek 1981; Miksicek 1991; Wing and Scudder 1991). Maize agriculture was documented from the beginning of occupation, and is now known to have been present in the Maya lowlands from probably the third millennium BC (Pohl *et al.* 1996). The people of Cuello genetically improved maize over the centuries to produce a broader cob with larger kernels, more productive per plant and per hectare (Miksicek *et al.* 1981; Miksicek 1991: Figure 4.1): such an increase would accord with the architectural and demographic evidence for expansion at the site (Wilk and Wilhite 1991). Beans (*Phaseolus* sp.) have a low apparent importance, on a par with tree crops such as avocado and *nance* (Miksicek 1991: Table 4.7), although preparation methods are likely to lead to low levels of preservation and underestimation of their real dietary contribution (Miksicek 1991: 78). A similar argument may be applied to root crops such as the sweet potato, or *camote* (*Ipomoea batatas*); manioc (cassava, yuca) (*Manihot esculenta*); and *malanga* (yautia) (*Xanthosoma* spp.). Bronson (1966) suggested the supplementation of maize with root crops, by which agricultural yield would be sufficiently increased and nutritionally enhanced to meet the needs of a population of greater density than would be possible under a standard maize-farming regime. Bronson considered that documentary and botanical evidence for four crops – those above and yam bean, or *jícama* (*Pachyrrhizus erosus*) – suggested that the Maya region was a centre for either domestication or diversification. He argued that the Maya had a variety of root crops available to them before the colonial age and arguably in the Classic Period. Marcus (1982) argued instead for a much later, post-Columbian introduction of three of these root crops, while admitting that a Classic Maya knowledge of wild roots and tubers, particularly for use as famine foods, may have been comprehensive. *Pachyrrhizus,* she suggests, was likely to have been a Postclassic (AD 900–1500) introduction and possibly a famine food.

While standard flotation techniques were adequate for recovering carbonized seeds such as maize, the parenchymatous tissue which forms the bulk of roots and tubers is destroyed by them. Manioc wood was known from Late Period Cuello (Miksicek 1991: Table 4.6), but only when new recovery techniques developed in the Pacific were applied by Hather (Hather and Hammond 1994) were root crops recovered at Cuello. Manioc, probably *malanga*, and possibly sweet potato were cultivated, either in the same fields as corn or in complementary patches, and were found in 60 per cent of the samples analysed. Although maize was probably the single most important plant food (see below), the Preclassic diet was very different in its emphases from that of the late prehispanic and colonial Maya.

In the same way that systematic recovery and study of plant remains from Cuello has clarified our view of prehispanic Maya agriculture, the evidence of animal remains has given a different picture of protein procurement. The broad study of Wing and Scudder (1991) showed that white-tailed deer (*Odocoileus virginianus*) provided slightly more than half the meat in the diet, both in terms of animal numbers and of flesh yield, followed by freshwater turtles (especially *Kinosternon* sp.), and then by dog (*Canis familiaris*). Other forest species, including brocket deer (*Mazama* sp.), peccary (*Tayassuidae*), large rodents and armadillos and other reptiles and birds, were minor contributors. Although neither the mortality pattern nor the skeletal morphology suggest that *Odocoileus* stood in a closer relationship to the Maya than that of hunted to hunter, the high proportion of juveniles in some cache offerings suggests some kind of selectivity. Similar selection, at the smaller end of the animal range, is seen in the shell sizes of the edible snail *Pomacea flagellata*, which was consistently collected at a perceived maturity/taste optimum of *c.* 38 millimetres in diameter (Miksicek 1991: Figure 4.2).

The one meat source that was certainly both controlled and fully domesticated was the dog: at the time of the Spanish conquest Francisco Hernández described a breed called *techichi* as being *Indis edulis*, 'eaten by the Indians', and in 1657 J. Jonston quoted Hernández, adding 'the Indians of Cozumel Island ate these dogs as the Spaniards do rabbits. Those intended for this purpose were castrated in order to fatten them.' (Quoted in Allen 1920: 483, 489–90.) Hamblin's (1984) study of Late Postclassic (AD 1250–1520) dogs on Cozumel concluded that most if not all of them were *techichi*; Carr (1986: 237–57) identified at least ninety-six dogs in the Preclassic sample from Cerros, some 50 kilometres from Cuello, with low variability suggesting a homogeneous population also approximating to *techichi*, and with an absence of the congenital dental

abnormalities which would have indicated the hairless *xoloitzcuintli* breed known to the Aztecs.

At Cuello some 600 domestic dog bones and teeth were found in all Preclassic periods (Wing and Scudder 1991: Table 1; Clutton-Brock and Hammond 1994: Tables 1-2), mixed in with other food remains, both plant and animal. While foot bones and teeth greatly outnumber the remainder of the skeleton, this is unlikely to signify a Maya preference for particular body parts, but much more likely to reflect the difficulty of distinguishing highly fragmented bones of small dogs from other mammals of the same size. While much of the breakage could have been caused by trampling, it is also possible that bones were crushed and boiled to extract marrow.

The paucity of deciduous teeth and the absence of unfused epiphyses indicates that few puppies were present: permanent dentition is in place by five months, while epiphyseal fusion is complete by ten months, indicating survival at least to nearly the end of the first year of life; but the unworn state of the teeth indicates that most of the dogs did not live for much longer. There is no evidence of any special diet, and the dogs would probably have eaten household scraps. The mortality pattern, of killing at around a year old, with no older individuals and few puppies present, is consistent with care of the litter until the first growth spurt was over and the animals could yield a reasonable amount of meat. Many of the limb bones appear to have been chopped or broken, presumably for extraction of the marrow; one atlas vertebra has a faint knife cut, made perhaps when the head was removed from the dog's body. Dog bones were also used in the same way as those from other meat-bearing species, in the manufacture of artefacts (cf. Hammond 1991: 180–83). In a society where hunting was the major means of acquiring protein, the availability of domesticated dogs, requiring low energy expenditure to breed, feed and butcher, formed a usefully reliable counterbalance to the vagaries of the chase.

These morphological and metrical studies of

dietary remains from Cuello are complemented by recent stable-isotope analyses of human and animal bones, which have enabled us to investigate a series of further questions. Among them were the extent to which maize was a staple, whether dogs were specifically raised as a food source and whether deer, the dominant meat source, were tamed or loose-herded. The social inequalities hinted at by burial patterns raised the question of whether differences in diet based on gender or status were evident at Cuello, and whether the diet of the apparent sacrificial victims in the mass burials was different from that of the rest of the population, giving some indication of social distinction from the rest of the burial population.

To resolve these questions, we measured the stable carbon and nitrogen isotope ratios in Preclassic human skeletons from Cuello, using collagen as the sample material, but also measuring the carbon isotopes in the apatite of bone and tooth enamel; we also analysed animal

bones from the archaeological deposits, and finally the bones and/or flesh of modern terrestrial, riverine and marine animals collected in the area in 1992 (Tykot *et al.* 1996). The carbon (^{13}C) and nitrogen (^{15}N) isotope ratios were measured in a mass spectrometer and reported using the delta notation in parts per thousand or per mil. Fig. 37 shows both humans and the archaeological fauna in boxes representing the means plus or minus one standard deviation. Clustering around -20 parts per mil for carbon are the deer, turtle and peccary. The collagen values of modern animals eating C3 plants are about 2 per mil more negative than those from the Preclassic and indicate that modern values cannot be used unchanged in any study of archaeological diets. Clearly, there is no evidence of maize in the diet of either the white-tailed or brocket deer, which would have suggested taming or loose-herding in the Preclassic: all the species seem to have lived in the forest or on its margins. The dogs, on the other hand, all had a substantial

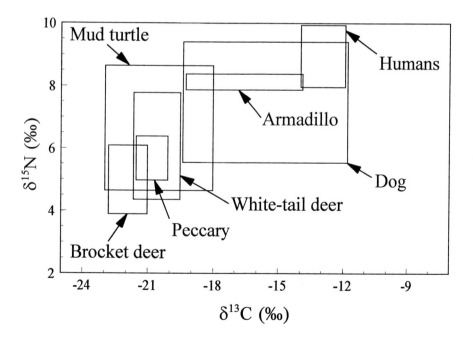

37 *Stable-isotope concentrations for humans and food animals at Cuello. Only humans and dogs have a high maize and protein intake, while deer and peccary are typical forest feeders.*

C4 component to their diet, about 40 per cent on average, although the high variability suggests that they were not fed a controlled diet but instead scavenged within the community, eating (as modern dogs do) food scraps and even human waste.

The humans at Cuello were significantly enriched in both carbon and nitrogen, as would be expected with a maize-based, omnivorous diet. There is spacing in carbon values between collagen and apatite: C4 carbon made up about 55 per cent of the collagen and 35 per cent of the apatite, a discrepancy best explained by the regular consumption of both dogs and armadillo, each with substantial C4 components to their own diets. There also seem to be small differences between males and females, evident in the carbon isotopes in both collagen and tooth enamel; one possible explanation is that the extra C4 in the male diet was acquired from the consumption of *chicha* maize beer.

Maize provided about 35 per cent of the nutritional intake overall: as yet, there is not enough evidence to suggest any chronological distinctions in the Preclassic diet from Swasey through to Cocos times. Some of the sacrificed individuals in the two mass burials, however, were either not native to the Cuello area or were fed significantly different diets for a significant part of their later life: either explanation is consonant with their being warriors, and the former with their being captives taken specifically for sacrifice in dedicatory rituals for the construction and later refurbishment of Platform 34.

Much more substantial differences have been documented for successive time periods in Belize. Fig. 38 combines the data for Preclassic Cuello with that for Late Preclassic/Classic Period Barton Ramie and Baking Pot, and Postclassic/Historic Lamanai. The general trend is intensification of maize consumption from Preclassic through Classic to Postclassic and Historic times, followed

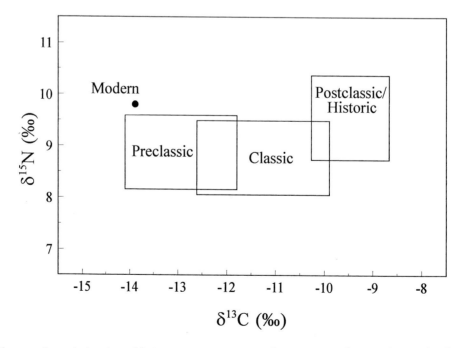

38 *Changes through time in stable-isotope concentrations for sites in northern and central Belize: while protein intake remains fairly constant over the 2,500 years from Preclassic Cuello to Postclassic/Historic Lamanai, relative maize consumption rises. Modern consumption is close to the Preclassic level.*

by a reduction in the modern era. Other work shows that people in Petexbatún and Usumacinta and at Copán in Honduras were considerably more dependent on maize than those in Belize, with those at Copán truly subsisting on a corn and beans diet. Unlike the situation in Belize, the wildlife and plant cover of the Copán valley were rapidly eradicated by growing populations during the Classic. In the Petén more meat was consumed, but they were still more dependent on maize than were populations of the same time in Belize who had access to a wider range of ecozones and presumably had a lower population density. It appears that geography and local ecology played a primary role in determining the diet of the ancient Maya.

Thus subsistence data complements the evidence of social development and ritual activity in defining the nature of early Maya culture. While the Cuello community itself was never important in the Maya political landscape, its study enables aspects of that landscape to be traced from their beginnings, and hence better understood. The foundations of Classic Maya economy and society, the infrastructure of the great cities such as Tikal,

Calakmul, Palenque and Copán, were laid in the Preclassic period in the establishment and growth of villages and small towns such as Cuello.

Acknowledgements

The recent work reported here was carried out in collaboration with Amanda Clarke, Sara Donaghey and Juliette Cartwright Gerhardt (excavations), Cynthia Robin, Julie M. Saul and Frank P. Saul (burials), Jon Hather (palaeobotany), Juliet Clutton-Brock (zooarchaeology), and Nikolaas Van Der Merwe and Robert H. Tykot (stable isotope analysis), building on that reported in Hammond 1991. Excavations since 1990 were funded by the National Geographic Society, Boston University, and an anonymous donor. Figs 33 and 36 are adapted from those used initially in my book *Ancient Maya Civilization* (Rutgers University Press/Cambridge University Press 1982), figs 34 and 35 are by Sheena Howarth (Cuello Project Archive, Boston University), and figs 37 and 38 are by Robert H. Tykot (from a collaborative project with myself and Nikolaas Van Der Merwe).

References

Allen, G.M. (1920) 'Dogs of the American Aborigines', *Bulletin of the Museum of Comparative Zoology, Harvard University*, 63, 431–517.

Andrews, E. Wyllys, v (1986) 'Olmec jades from Chacsinkin, Yucatan, and Maya ceramics from La Venta, Tabasco', *Research and Reflections in Archaeology and History: Essays in Honor of Doris Stone*, E. Wyllys Andrews v (ed.), 11–49. New Orleans: Tulane University, Middle American Research Institute, Publication 57.

Andrews, E. Wyllys, v (1987) 'A cache of early jades from Chacsinkin, Yucatan', *Mexicon* 9, 78–85.

Andrews, E. Wyllys, v, and Norman Hammond (1990) 'Redefinition of the Swasey Phase at Cuello, Belize', *American Antiquity* 54, 570–84.

Bronson, Bennet (1966) 'Roots and the subsistence of the ancient Maya', *Southwestern Journal of Anthropology* 22, 251–79.

Carr, H.S. (1986) 'Faunal Utilization in a Late Preclassic Maya Community at Cerros, Belize'. Ph.D. Thesis. Tulane University.

Cliff, M. B. (1988) 'Domestic architecture and origins of complex society at Cerros', *Household and Community in the Mesoamerican Past*, R.R. Wilk and W. Ashmore (eds), 199–225. Albuquerque: University of New Mexico Press.

Clutton-Brock, Juliet and Norman Hammond (1994) 'Hot dogs: Comestible canids in Preclassic Maya culture at Cuello, Belize', *Journal of Archaeological Science* 21, 819–26.

Collier, George (1975) *Fields of the Tzotzil*. Austin: University of Texas Press.

Hamblin, N.L. (1984) *Animal Use by the Cozumel Maya*. Tucson: University of Arizona Press.

Hammond, Norman (ed.) (1991) *Cuello: An early*

Maya community in Belize. Cambridge: Cambridge University Press.

Hammond, Norman and Juliette Cartwright Gerhardt (1990) 'Early Maya architectural innovation at Cuello, Belize', *World Archaeology* 21, 461–81.

Hammond, Norman and Charles H. Miksicek (1981) 'Ecology and economy of a Formative Maya site at Cuello, Belize', *Journal of Field Archaeology* 8, 259–69.

Hammond, Norman, Amanda Clarke and Francisco Estrada Belli (1992) 'Middle Preclassic Maya buildings and burials at Cuello, Belize', *Antiquity* 66, 955–64.

Hammond, Norman, Amanda Clarke and Sara Donaghey (1995) 'The long goodbye: Middle Preclassic Maya archaeology at Cuello, Belize', *Latin American Antiquity* 6, 120–28.

Hammond, Norman, Amanda Clarke and Cynthia Robin (1991) 'Middle Preclassic Buildings and Burials at Cuello, Belize: 1990 Investigations', *Latin American Antiquity* 2, 352–63.

Hather, Jon G., and Norman Hammond (1994) 'Ancient Maya subsistence diversity: root and tuber remains from Cuello, Belize', *Antiquity* 68: 330–35, 487–8.

Haviland, William A. (1985) *Excavations in Small Residential Groups of Tikal: Groups 4F-1 and 4F-2. Tikal Report 19*. Philadelphia: University Museum, University of Pennsylvania.

Housley, Rupert A., Norman Hammond and Ian Law (1991) 'AMS radiocarbon dating of Preclassic Maya burials at Cuello, Belize', *American Antiquity* 56, 514–19.

Kosakowsky, Laura J. (1987) *Prehistoric Maya Pottery at Cuello, Belize*. Anthropological Paper 47. Tucson: University of Arizona Press.

Law, Ian, Rupert A. Housley, Norman Hammond and Robert E. M. Hedges (1991) 'Cuello: Resolving the chronology through direct dating of conserved and low-collagen bone by AMS', *Radiocarbon* 33, 303–15.

Marcus, Joyce (1982) 'The plant world of the Sixteenth- and Seventeenth-Century Maya', *Maya Subsistence: Studies in Memory of Dennis E. Puleston*, K.V. Flannery (ed.), 239–67. New York: Academic Press.

McAnany, Patricia A. (1995) *Living with the Ancestors*. Austin: University of Texas Press.

Miksicek, Charles H. (1991) 'The ecology and economy of Cuello: I, the natural and cultural landscape of Preclassic Cuello', *Cuello: An Early Maya Community in Belize*, N. Hammond (ed.), 70–84. Cambridge: Cambridge University Press.

Miksicek, Charles H., Robert. M. Bird, Barbara Pickersgill, Sara Donaghey, Juliette Cartwright and Norman Hammond (1981) 'Preclassic lowland maize from Cuello, Belize' *Nature* 289, 56–9.

Pohl, Mary D., Kevin O. Pope, John G. Jones, John S. Jacob, Dolores R. Piperno, Susan D. deFrance, David L. Lentz, John A. Gifford, Marie E. Danforth and J. Kathryn Josserand (1996) 'Early Agriculture in the Maya Lowlands', *Latin American Antiquity* 7: 355–72.

Sharer, Robert J. and David W. Sedat (1987) *Archaeological Investigations in the Northern Maya Highlands, Guatemala*. Philadelphia: University Museum, University of Pennsylvania.

Tykot, Robert H., Nikolaas Van Der Merwe and Norman Hammond (1996) 'Stable Isotope Analysis of Bone Collagen, Bone Apatite, and Tooth Enamel in the Reconstruction of Human Diet. A Case Study from Cuello, Belize', *Archaeological Chemistry: Organic, Inorganic, and Biochemical Analysis* (ACS Symposium Series 625), Mary Virginia Orna (ed.), 355–65. Washington DC: American Chemical Society.

Wilk, Richard R. and Harold L. Wilhite Jr. (1991) 'The community of Cuello: Patterns of household and settlement change', *Cuello: An Early Maya Community in Belize*, N. Hammond (ed.), 118–33. Cambridge: Cambridge University Press.

Willey, Gordon R., William R. Bullard, Jr., John B. Glass and James C. Gifford (1965) *Prehistoric Maya Settlements in the Belize Valley*. Paper of the Peabody Museum of Archaeology and Ethnology, Harvard University, 54. Cambridge, MA: Peabody Museum.

Wing, Elizabeth S. and Sylvia J. Scudder (1991) 'The exploitation of animals', *Cuello: An Early Maya Community in Belize*, N. Hammond (ed.), 84–97. Cambridge: Cambridge University Press.

1 *View of Teotihuacan's core from the Moon Plaza to the south, with the Street of the Dead in the centre and the Pyramid of the Sun to the left.* (Photo: Linda Manzanilla)

2 *Theatre-type censer found around Burial 8 at the Oztoyahualco compound in Teotihuacan (Manzanilla 1993; Manzanilla and Carreón 1991).* (Photo: Linda Manzanilla)

3 *Two dog skeletons near Burials 20 and 21 in the 'Cueva del Pirul' tunnel at Teotihuacan.* (Photo: Linda Manzanilla)

4 *View of the Temple of the Feathered Serpent, Teotihuacan.* (Photo: Linda Manzanilla)

Opposite 5 *Sculpture of Mictlantecuhtli, 'Lord of the World of the Dead', found in the House of Eagles, Tenochtitlan, in September 1994. The stucco loincloth that the image had when it was discovered has not yet been restored.* (Photo: Saturnino Vallejo, courtesy of INAH)

6 *Facade of the House of Eagles, Tenochtitlan, partially buried under Justo Sierra Street and the Porrúa bookshop.* (Photo: Ignacio Guevara, courtesy of INAH)

7 *Offering 16 at the Templo Mayor is a cosmogram that represents the five regions of the earth's surface. It is dominated by the image of Xiuhtecuhtli, 'Lord of the Year' and Fire God.* (Photo: Salvador Guilliem, courtesy of INAH)

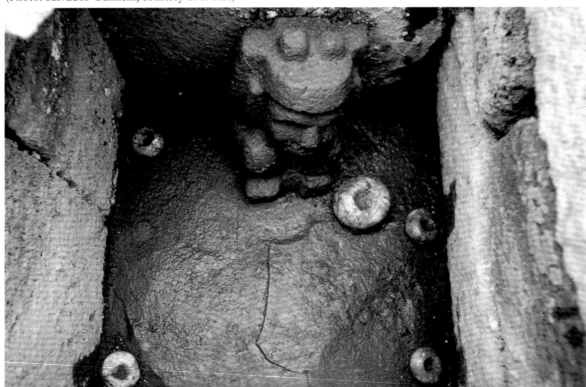

8 *Phonetic elements in toponyms.*
Upper row: Tonalla, Tenextlacotla,
Aphiyoca, Mallinaloca, Chipiltepec,
Telpochmilpa.
Lower row: Tena(n)co, Chiyapolco,
Tetepantla.
These are small communities subject to
rulers of Tepetlaoztoc. Repeated
Náhuatl sound elements include the
clay-coloured pot (co-), lips (te(n)-),
stone (te-), hand (ma-), the red flag
(pan-), arrow tip (mi-), tooth gum
(tla(n)), blue water (a-) and white chia
flour (chi-). In some cases, e.g. the lime
(stone-ash)-rod of Tenextlacotla,
rendered as ash, lip, tooth, pot, tooth,
phonetics prevail over concept.
Tepetlaoztoc Codex f.5. (Photo ©
British Museum; BM Add. MSS 13964
Kingsborough f.207r)

9 *Glyph for Huaxtepec. Plumed*
Serpent Pyramid, Xochicalco. (Photo:
Gordon Brotherston)

10 *Glyph for Tepeyahualco. Cuauhtinchan Map 1.*

11 *Xolotl Map, left half.*

Opposite 12 *Before the 1910 Revolution, the great estates* (haciendas) *had a profound impact on the lives of many indigenous people, taking away communal lands and irrigation water.* (Photo: John Gledhill)

13 *Mass at a hilltop chapel in the community of Patamban, Michoacán. Even young Purhépecha women still wear the traditional shawl* (rebozo). (Photo: John Gledhill)

14 *The home of a Purhépecha family in the Meseta Tarasca region of Michoacán. Illegal logging by community 'bosses' and outsiders has diminished the rich communal forest resources of Purhépecha communities and is a major source of local conflict.* (Photo: John Gledhill)

15–16 *Decorating the streets in memory of the dead, Patamban, Michoacán.* (Photos: John Gledhill)

17–18 *Migrant cane cutters from Náhuatl-speaking communities in Guerrero state, photographed in the housing provided for them in the village of Los Limones, Michoacán. The 'galleries' had earth floors, and the families slept on the straw mats seen rolled up in the background (below).*
(Photos: Kathy Powell)

19 *The main trench at Cuello in 1980, seen from the southeast, with the pyramid Structure 350 of c.* AD *250 at left and Middle Preclassic buildings under excavation in the foreground.* (Photo: Norman Hammond – Cuello Project)

20 *Part of Mass Burial 1 of c. 400* BC, *including a skull with unhealed puncture wound and part of a detached humerus (lower right).* (Photo: Norman Hammond – Cuello Project)

21 *Marine shell beads from child Burial 152, of c. 700 BC. The red beads are made from the valued thorny oyster* Spondylus americanus, *the white ones probably from* Strombus, *and form part of a skein of more than 500 beads, suggesting inherited wealth.* (Photo: Norman Hammond – Cuello Project)

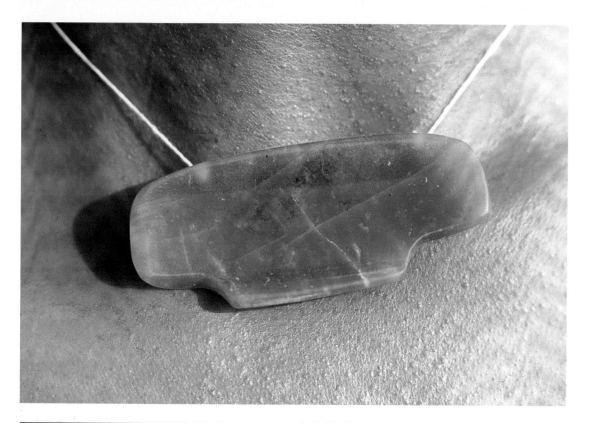

22 *Blue jade pendant of c. 600 BC, from child Burial 166. The concave front represents a metallic-ore mirror of Olmec type, and the object may be an Olmec artefact.* (Photo: Norman Hammond – Cuello Project)

23 *Bone gorget, made from a disc of human skull, with cut-out eyes and mouth and two suspension holes. Burial 160, c. 500–450 BC.* (Photo: Norman Hammond – Cuello Project)

Left 24 *Seated pottery figure, Olmec, 1200–400 BC (H. 15.5 cm). Hollow figures, made from a white kaolin clay, are characteristically Olmec, and their sporadic appearance far from the Gulf Coast (e.g. in central Mexico) is usually interpreted as evidence of contact with the Olmec world. (Photo © British Museum; Ethno. 1981 Am 27.1)*

25 *Pottery whistle-figurine in the shape of a woman carrying a child, Classic period (H. 15.7 cm). She wears a mantle (quexquémitl) decorated with birds painted in red, and a black pigment made from a mixture of rubber and tar covers parts of her face and headdress. Bitumen occurs naturally in the oil-rich zones of the Gulf Coast, and the use of this material (chapopote) is characteristic of figurines from Veracruz. (Photo © British Museum; Ethno. 1977 Am 38.1)*

26 *Pottery 'smiling head', broken from a complete figure, Veracruz Late Classic period (H. 14 cm). Smiling figures were made in moulds, with details added by hand. They represent young men or women in a standing posture with the arms outstretched, and are usually found in tombs and offerings. (Photo © British Museum; Ethno. 1975 Am 8.3)*

27 *Panel 6, South Ballcourt, El Tajín. The walls of the main ballcourt at this site are decorated with a series of carved reliefs illustrating the rituals and ceremonies associated with the game. Panel 6 depicts a sacrifice by decapitation, and the principal figures wear ball-game costumes. The volute designs around the borders are typical of Tajín art.* (Photo: Aline Magnoni)

28 *Pottery incense burner, Isla de Sacrificios,* AD 900–1521 *(H. 9 cm). This item is part of a collection obtained from the site by Capt. Evan Nepean, a British naval officer, whose material has been in the British Museum since 1844* (Photo © British Museum; Ethno. 1844.7-20.931)

6. The Gulf Coast Cultures and the Recent Archaeological Discoveries at El Manatí, Veracruz

Ponciano Ortíz Ceballos and Ma. del Carmen Rodríguez

The area encompassed by the present-day state of Veracruz and neighbouring Tabasco, San Luis Potosí and Hidalgo was the homeland for important groups of people who produced a rich material culture and contributed to the development of other Mesoamerican societies at different evolutionary stages.

It has traditionally been accepted that three main cultural groups developed in the Gulf Coast area of Mexico: Huastecs, Totonacs and Olmecs, occupying the north, centre and south of Veracruz respectively. However, these were not the only groups, as the great linguistic variety that existed at the time of Conquest indicates that the area was made up of a multiethnic mosaic. The names of these cultural or 'ethnic' groups were given by Spanish chroniclers at the time but possibly also refer to territories. In the light of what we are studying, it would be risky to assume that the earliest cultural remains of the Classic and Formative Periods correspond to the same groups, and to a unilinear development. For example, the so-called Formative 'Olmec' culture has little or nothing to do with the groups that the documentary sources call Xicalanca Olmecs and Uixtotin Olmecs.

This is obviously not the place to enter into a retrospective discussion on these groups; however, the matter must be noted in order to avoid future confusion. We will try to give a general explanation of the development of these societies in cultural horizons, or phases, while remaining aware that they may be modified or changed from one region to another.

Nomadic groups and the first settlements

As for other parts of Mesoamerica, information is scarce regarding the way of life on the Gulf Coast during the Preceramic period. We have dates from only three sites, the first situated in the lower Tecolutla River basin (the site of Santa Luisa), the second in the lower Actopan and Colipa River basin, primarily from a site known as Rancho Nuevo, and the third from the Tamaulipeca mountain range. The earliest date in Veracruz comes from Santa Luisa, the so-called Conchita complex dating to 5600 BC, and the Palo Hueco phase that spans a period from 4000 to 2400 BC (Wilkerson 1972, 1981). The site of Rancho Nuevo has not been excavated: information comes from surface collections (Medellín 1975: 87).

The tools found at Santa Luisa consisted of small obsidian flakes, awls, chisels, scrapers and fire-cracked stones, plus other artefacts indicative of nomadic groups who established temporary campsites, or of semi-nomads with an economy based upon extensive exploitation of produce from the rivers, estuaries and sea, no doubt complemented by hunting and the gathering of tubers (Wilkerson 1981).

At Rancho Nuevo there is an artefact assemblage similar to that of Santa Luisa, including fire-cracked stones, hand axes, grinders, scrapers, knives, stone vessels, chisels and obsidian projectile points (percussion flaked and retouched), which bear a resemblance to objects from the Tehuacán Valley and are, therefore, datable to between 4000 and 2000 BC. These artefacts would also pertain to nomadic bands and semi-nomadic gatherers, hunters and fishers (Medellín 1975: 88). A similar artefact complex has been reported in the Sierra de Tamaulipas, today in Huastec territory, which corresponds to the phases named Diablo and Lerma that date between 9000 and 7000 BC, followed by La Nogales, La Perra and Almagre which span a period from 4200 to 2500 BC (MacNeish 1954, 1958; Ekholm 1944).

The emergence of small villages: the Formative or Preclassic period

The Early Formative period is characterized by the emergence of small villages or permanent settlements; the invention, or introduction, of pottery; and by an increase in cultural material. The earliest evidence is again from the site of Santa Luisa in the lower Tecolutla basin. The earliest phase, dating between 1700 and 1450 BC, is known as Raudal and is followed by the Almería phase, dating from 1450 to 1350 BC (Wilkerson 1981).

At this time the inhabitants of the Tecolutla basin were making globular, narrow-mouthed vessels for use in food preparation and small jars decorated with red slip, spiral-shaped incisions and vertical grooves. Among the stone tools are a great number of small retouched obsidian flakes apparently used for processing manioc and other tubers, and basalt vessels for pulping vegetables. These materials tie in very well with dates from the Barra and Locona phases of Chiapas (Ceja 1985; Lowe 1975; Clark 1989), with which they are contemporary. This could indicate a similarity in basic subsistence patterns between the Gulf and Pacific coasts.

The quantity of small obsidian flakes has given rise to suggestions of a subsistence based mainly upon the consumption of tubers and a preparation of vegetables and legumes, such as chillies, tomatoes, squash and beans. Maize was probably not eaten in the form of *tortillas*, as grinding stones (*metates*) dating to this period have not been found. In the later Monte Gordo and Ojite phases at Santa Luisa, local communities were influenced by the Olmec complex.

In the lower Coatzacoalcos River basin at San Lorenzo Tenochtitlan, material corresponding to the Early Formative, 1500–1200 BC, has also been reported (Coe and Diehl 1980). As at Santa Luisa, the characteristics of this cultural material relate to the early phases of Chiapas and the Pacific coast and therefore socioeconomic organization could be similar in all these areas. Recent excavations at San Lorenzo Tenochtitlan are revealing important information that will increase our present knowledge of this outstanding site (Cyphers 1995a and b).

Information recently obtained from El Manatí, Veracruz, also shows evidence of an occupation with ceramic and lithic material similar to that of Chiapas and San Lorenzo, although this is a ceremonial site, and the food consumed there could have been related to ritual customs. However, the link is obvious; more importantly it is associated with ritual offerings of axes and rubber balls, amongst other elements, indicating a clearly defined 'Olmec' pattern. Two radiocarbon dates obtained from the earliest deposits associated with the ceramics give a date of 1400 BC, confirming that from this early age Olmec elements were already incorporated into this ceremony (Ortíz and Rodríguez 1995).

The fundamental change: the emergence of civilization

Around 1200 BC a series of economic and social changes happened which served to modify the previous cultural pattern. While, as yet, we do not have clear archaeological evidence as to how this development took place, we know that the inhabitants of ancient villages began to organize and plan their constructions, creating sacred, political and social spaces. Large population centres grew up, allowing the structuring of an economy with production surpluses and the creation of a large network of commercial interchange. These helped forge the 'Olmec' culture – the first 'state' or civilization in Mesoamerica, which has been considered the 'mother culture'

(Caso 1942; Covarrubias 1942, 1946, 1956).

Due to a lack of stone in the region, temples and houses were constructed from earth and clay and, although modest, showed the model for future Mesoamerican architecture during the Classic period. Spatial planning was based upon a knowledge of astronomy, and at sites like San Lorenzo and La Venta one can recognize an ideology that formed the basis of later Mesoamerican religion (Drucker 1952a, 1952b; Drucker, Heizer and Squier 1959; González 1995). In the same way, their conception of nature and the supernatural was represented by the sacred stones of jade and basalt, the first a symbol of water and the second of volcanoes and fire, elements present throughout ancient Mexican history.

The beautiful monumental sculptures of these people are surprising; the colossal heads, altars and anthropomorphic figures show a delicacy and craftsmanship never equalled in the working of fine-grained stones, jade and serpentine, in which a rich symbolism can be seen relating to customs, beliefs and religious practices (fig. 39). The cult of nature, ancestors and their descendants, the child 'gods', formed the basis of religion, and these factors were tied to the water cult (springs and rain), hills, caves, forests, impressive flora and powerful animals. For example, tigers, crocodiles and snakes are mixed with human images, and the 'child god' cult, the symbol of rain, birth and fertility, predominates. The need to reproduce images in a colossal and magnificent way indicates a people eager to show its power and greatness, but also one that was finally overwhelmed by its pride.

At this time (the Middle Formative/Preclassic), elements of Olmec culture made their way, directly or indirectly, to many other parts of Mexico, where they appeared intrusively in local cultures alongside the regional artefacts. For example, certain elements cross the area between the Gulf Coast proper to the south of Central America, northwards to the Valley of Mexico and from the Pacific coast to Morelos (Chalcatzingo; Grove 1987) and Guerrero (Teopantecuanitlan; Martínez

Donjuán 1986). It is interesting that in the majority of cases, each region, each site and each space has its own unique personality.

Paradoxically, considering the importance of trying to understand the growth of this civilization, only a few sites from the nuclear 'Olmec' area of Veracruz have been excavated with any degree of detail, and not all have been fully reported: San Lorenzo (Coe and Diehl 1980), Tres Zapotes (Drucker 1943b), Laguna de los

39 *Votive jade figure, Olmec, 1200–400 BC (H. 29 cm). Plain axes, and figures based on axe-like shapes, occur in Olmec offerings and caches. The cleft head, flame-shaped eyebrows and toothless downturned mouth are diagnostic features of the Olmec style, in which human and animal features are blended into a single image, perhaps the representation of a deity. (Photo © British Museum; Ethno. St. 536)*

Cerros and, in the last few years, Las Limas, El Mayacal and El Manatí in Veracruz, and La Venta in Tabasco. Recently, David Grove and Susan Gillespie undertook work in a community named La Isla, an area close to Laguna de los Cerros, that contributed interesting information on a Late Formative village (although it also has Classic period occupation). In addition, they carried out work in a sculpture workshop which had previously been reported by Medellín in the 1960s (Grove 1994; Gillespie 1994).

The 'Olmec' horizon or tradition can be recognized in practically all of Veracruz. It is identified principally by its ceramic style, its forms and decorative motifs, and by the unmistakable and equally important 'baby-face' figurines (col. pl. 24) present in excavated sites in the Sierra de Los Tuxtlas (Ortíz and Santley 1988), Mixtequilla (Drucker 1943; Stark 1986, 1989), Trapiche, Chalahuite, Limoncito, Viejón with its important stela (García Payón 1966; Lira 1982), Las Higueras (Arellanos 1985), Santa Luisa (Wilkerson 1972), Xalapa (Medellín 1975), and Tabuco (Ortíz and Aquino 1978, 1987), today in Huastec territory. In addition, of course, this Olmec tradition is found in almost all of Mesoamerica, especially at Tlatilco in the Basin of Mexico.

The Olmec collapse

After 900 BC, due to unknown causes, Olmec society lost strength and vitality. Evidence of a revolution can be seen at San Lorenzo. The people, tired of submission to the hard labour required to maintain its grandeur, rebelled. This suggestion, made by Bernal (1975: 233), could be a valid argument, provided that the simulated, or symbolic, destruction of the town's monuments was not provoked by foreign invaders or rituals with as yet unknown meanings (Grove 1981).

These changes might also have been influenced by certain ecological factors caused primarily by volcanic eruptions in southern Veracruz. We know that at least three violent eruptions took place

during ancient times – one in the Early Formative, another in the Protoclassic and one more in the Classic period – which would have covered the whole Tuxtla region, and probably further afield, with lava and ash (Ortíz 1975; Santley, Ortíz and Pool 1987). These events would have brought about abrupt changes in the weather, soils, flora and fauna, and would no doubt have caused large population centres to move. The effects of these phenomena have not really been evaluated but do perhaps help to explain some of the cultural changes these settlements underwent.

We believe that the loss of power and control by the Olmecs was gradual rather than abrupt, since their knowledge survived and was accepted by the cultures of Classic period Mesoamerica. The growth of other towns both within and outside the region reduced its power, and opportunities arose for other centres and cultures to draw political and economic control away from the area.

Between 300 BC and AD 300 some towns developed a custom inherited from the Olmecs and began to represent important events in stone, not only myths, but also when, how and where historic events took place. These include stelae found at Tres Zapotes (Stirling 1943, 1965), and in particular the important Stela C, which dates, according to correlation A, to 4 November 291 BC and, according to B, to 2 September AD 31. This stela and the figurine from Los Tuxtlas dating to 98 BC or AD 162, plus those from Cerro de Las Mesas and El Mesón and those from Izapa in Chiapas, are proof that there was a knowledge of a calendar linked with narrative scenes, an obvious legacy of the Olmec culture.

A recently discovered stela at a site called La Mojarra in the district of Alvarado, Veracruz, is shedding light upon writing, sociopolitical events, and the use of the calendar. It is also shedding light on the language that was spoken at the time, which appears to support earlier suppositions that it was Protozoque or Zoque (Stuart 1993; Justesen and Kaufman 1993).

The Classic period: the Mesoamerican climax

Between the years AD 300 to 900, a number of peoples occupying the area between the hills and the coastal lowlands, as in other parts of Mesoamerica, began to differentiate, and achieved notable advances in social, political and religious order. There is no doubt that this was made possible thanks to the development of cultivation techniques allowing food surpluses, together with the securing of raw materials and other goods that strengthened long-distance trade. Religion also had a vital importance; the life of these towns revolved around it.

During the Early Classic, from AD 300 to 600, several towns evolved and transformed into ceremonial centres. The centre and southern part of the state was inhabited by groups that exchanged goods, services and ideas with the central highlands, especially with Teotihuacan. The most important sites in central Veracruz at this time were Remojadas, Trapiche, Chalahuite, Limoncito Tolome, El Tejar, El Faisán, Nopiloa, Los Cerros and Dicha Tuerta, among others (Medellín 1953, 1960, 1975; Daneels 1988). Ceremonial centres were built of earth, mud and adobe (sometimes plastered) with burnt earth floors, since, like other towns in the southern lowlands, they lacked suitable building stone.

Clay sculptures from this period have a realistic nature and are predominantly hollow, medium sized and superbly finished. The principal figures are women wearing elegant costumes, some with skirts, some without. Others have naked torsos and are adorned with necklaces and earrings (Medellín 1960, 1975). There are depictions of warriors armed with sword-clubs, shields and helmets, their faces painted black or covered with masks made of bitumen. Also emphasized are large-nosed gods that appear to represent the Sun, and there are the first representations of gods such as Xipe, Tlazoltéotl and the Cihuateteo. Certain customs, like the use of tar for teeth painting, are also present.

Teotihuacan influence can be seen in the doll-like figurines with triangular faces and large ear ornaments and the cylindrical tripod vessels that appear at various sites in central and northern Veracruz. However, of the sites explored to date, the one that has an undeniable Teotihuacan presence is Matacapan. Situated in a valley in the Sierra de los Tuxtlas, between San Andrés and Catemaco, it was first excavated in the 1940s by Juan Valenzuela and Karl Ruppert and then in the 1970s by the Tuxtla Olmec Project which undertook brief explorations in the area (Ortíz 1975). During the 1980s Robert Santley and Ponciano Ortíz reinitiated investigations in this zone, which, unfortunately, was recently severely damaged by the owners of the land through the introduction of an irrigation system and levelling of the ground for planting tobacco.

Recent information (Santley and Ortíz 1985; Santley, Ortíz and Pool 1987; Ortíz and Santley 1988) indicates that between AD 400 and 700 a Teotihuacan enclave was established at this site, which would have controlled the movement of its merchandise and of certain local materials (kaolin-rich clays, basalt, river, lacustrine and marine products and so on). This presence is suggested by an artefact complex that forms part of their ritual paraphernalia, like the cylindrical tripod vessels, figurines, *candeleros*, incense burners and also domestic and culinary wares. The majority of these objects are imitations and were made with local clay, copying Teotihuacan techniques and patterns. At least two of the temples in the area were constructed in the *talud-tablero* style and painted red (Valenzuela 1945a and b).

During the Late Classic period, AD 900–1200, several towns in the Veracruz region came to the end of their main developmental stage, a number of them showing signs that they had already attained their full potential.

In the Mixtequilla area, particularly at El Zapotal, clay-working reached its highest level of achievement, shown in the impressive sculpture of the god Mictlantecuhtli and the large quantity of

40 *Skulls and pottery figurines from a secondary burial at El Zapotal, Veracruz, Late Classic period. The 'smiling face' figurines are associated with the god Mictlantecuhtli.*

associated monumental sculptures, such as the impressive Cihuateteo, women who died during childbirth, which were used in a great ritual accompanied by a large number of sacrifices (fig. 40) (Ortega 1981). In direct contrast to this elaborate event is the relatively modest architecture at the site, constructed of clay and adobe. Due to the absence of stone these structures are now reduced to pyramid-shaped mounds of earth, occasionally covered with rough, uncut stones (Torres 1970, 1972).

In the semi-arid central region, as defined by the expert Medellín Zenil, the cities which were already established grew and expanded. The major art form was expressed in clay, as exemplified by the female figurines richly dressed in skirts and *quexquémitl* capes with exquisite multicoloured borders (col. pl. 25). Little study has been made of this rich, ancient ethnography, which comes from

sites like Nopiloa, Los Cerros and Dicha Tuerta and also bears a certain similarity to Maya figurines from Jaina in Campeche (Medellín 1953, 1960, 1987); many examples are unfortunately in foreign museums.

The 'smiling faces' are another well-known set of sculptures characteristic of central Veracruz (col. pl. 26), as are 'yokes' (fig. 41), votive *hachas* and *palmas*. Although yokes made their first appearance in the earliest part of the Formative, the quality of work attained a particular elegance and sophistication during the Classic period. This type of sculpture was used in funerary contexts and also apparently associated with the ball game.

Examples of *palmas* that show extraordinary workmanship are those salvaged by Arellanos and Beauregard in Banderilla, Veracruz (1981), and now exhibited in the Museum of Xalapa. An almost filigree-like quality is achieved in stone

41 *Stone yoke, Veracruz Classic period (H. 12 cm, W. 39.5 cm). Ball-game players are often depicted with 'yokes' (U-shaped protective belts) around their waists, though the heavy stone versions could never have functioned, and must have been replaced by equivalents made of lighter materials once the game began. The decoration on this example probably represents an Earth Monster. (Photo © British Museum; Ethno. St. 398)*

with representations of priests or, like those excavated by Wilkerson and Ortíz at Santa Luisa, bird forms, which are more modest although equally elegant and well finished. These objects were found associated with a yoke and are among the few examples recovered from documented archaeological contexts (Wilkerson 1970).

Pictorial art from this period is represented by the murals found at the site of Higueras and those recently excavated at El Tajín (Medellín 1979; Arellanos 1985; Brüggeman, Ladrón and Bonilla 1992). Scenes showing people in fabulous attire, an individual reclining in the sea pursued by sharks, and people playing trumpets and shells are a few examples of the civil and religious ceremonies seen in the stratigraphic sequence of plasterwork.

According to the archaeologist Medellín Zenil (1976: 43), 'under the direct influence of El Tajín, the Late Classic artists of Acacalco created a painted version of the stone reliefs seen at the large ceremonial centre, particularly the famous ball courts showing the feathered serpent, expressive human faces with similar nasal ornaments and priests wearing sun discs on their chests'. Furthermore, the earliest murals show a

Teotihuacan influence, such as floors painted dark red on light red with depictions of the feathered serpent and the *cipactli* (a crocodile-like creature, which also served as a calendrical day-sign). By the Late Classic certain deities are already easily distinguishable, such as Mictlantecuhtli, Tláloc, Xipe, Yacatecuhtli, Xochipilli, Xochiquetzal and Xólotl.

Undoubtedly the biggest exponent of the Late Classic world was El Tajín, founded as the governing centre of a large part of today's central and northern Veracruz. This enormous city extended over an area larger than 1,000 hectares; the core alone covers 100 hectares according to a rough survey carried out by Arellanos and Ortíz in 1978. It developed between AD 300 and 900 but, according to archaeologists, its florescence was from AD 900 to 1100 (García Payón 1942, 1951, 1971; Wilkerson 1980, 1987; Ortíz and Arellanos 1986; Brüggemann 1987a, 1992; Kampen 1972).

Traditionally it has been thought that the city was built by the Totonacs, but recent investigations highlight the possibility that it was actually Huastec (Wilkerson 1972). Its importance also lies in the actual style of its architecture, unique in Mesoamerica, in particular the elaborate

42 *Pyramid of the Niches, El Tajín. This temple platform, with its step-fret designs and 365 niches (one for each day of the year), was originally painted in black and red. The site of El Tajín has a long history, but attained its maximum power and political influence between* AD *900 and 1100. (Photo: Aline Magnoni)*

and sophisticated relief sculpture seen on the columns, panels and friezes that adorn ball courts (col. pl. 27), temples and palaces dedicated to the gods of wind, hurricanes and violent storms. The main pyramid, called the 'Pyramid of the Niches', was decorated with *grecas* (geometric step-fret designs) or *xicalcoliuhquis*, niches, facade panels and cornices, all integrated in a balanced harmony of dark and light and creating a contrast repeated in other constructions (fig. 42). Apparently the pyramid was originally painted black and red.

Six preserved columns carved with ritual scenes celebrating the deeds of one of the rulers of El Tajín, Thirteen Rabbit, form part of the Temple of the Columns and its annexes, and are examples of another monument type. Also depicted are warriors, divinities and animals. This building has an impressive flat roof, a feature seen on other structures and unique to El Tajín.

The city had a considerable number of ball courts: recent explorations directed by Dr Brüggemann have revealed more than ten of them. Another construction is the Xicalcoliuhqui, impressive for its almost monolithic architecture

made up of perfectly assembled blocks. The iconography of the relief carvings suggests the existence of a pantheon with deities such as Ometecuhtli, Mictlantecuhtli and Yacatecuhtli already present; we also know that the people of El Tajín used a calendar and a vigesimal numerical system expressed as bars and dots.

Although later than other Classic period towns, El Tajín also succumbed, through unknown causes, to violence. The city was burned, although it is not known if this was by outsiders or, following a revolt, by the inhabitants themselves (Wilkerson 1987: 73). Medellín (1976: 56) says 'the wise priests, who controlled large groups of people who had barely enough to satisfy their most immediate and urgent needs, became more and more sophisticated, behaving like manifestations of divinity itself, indicated by the magnificent way they were represented in painting and sculpture. The weight of their power and attire finished by overwhelming them. The priests had become removed from nature and social justice, resulting in popular revolt against oppressive theocracy throughout Mesoamerica'.

43 *The central plaza at Cempoala with on the left the Temple of Chimneys, so-called because of the chimney-like remains of circular columns on the platform at the base of the main stairway.*

The Postclassic, the resurrection and death of towns

Between AD 1200 and 1521 several settlements regained power and new cities were built, but with changes in political, territorial and social organization. Whole communities withdrew to the mountains and other places of difficult access, creating fortified centres. Others stayed on the coastal plains, vulnerable to domination by militarized peoples, who extorted tribute to sustain their lords, and slaves to satisfy the gods, who, in their turn, required more sacrificial blood to placate their anger. These warrior groups subjugated other settlements through fear and repression, and although some resisted, they were defeated in the end and later allied themselves to the Spanish conquistadors, thinking the Europeans would free them from this yoke.

Mentioned in the chronicles is the presence of foreign groups such as Nonoalcas, Toltecs, Pipiles and Xicalanca Olmec, among others. According to Medellín (1976: 22), in the document known as *Historia Tolteca-Chichimeca* and in the works of Muñoz Camargo are accounts of how Tula conquered several coastal towns like Coaxtla, Cempoala, Quiahuiztlan and Castillo de Teayo. Also mentioned are conquests by the Maltrata and Coscomatepec Chichimecs in the years 1176 and 1187 and later of the towns in the Orizaba and Perote regions such as Tlacolulan, Quiahuiztlan and Xicochimalco. These invasions forced other towns, like Centla and Comapan, to withdraw and build forts.

An important cultural complex known as Mixteca-Puebla, consisting of ceramics and figurines, is present at the sites of Maltrata, Ahuilizapan, Palmillas, Cotaxtla, Cuauhtochco, Cerro Grande, Madereros and Cerro de las Mesas. Imported ceramics or local imitations of foreign styles, such as Cholulteca or the so-called Aztec III, are present at these sites and are also seen at Cempoala, Quiahuiztlan, Isla de Sacrificios, Vega de la Peña, Morelos Paxil, Manantiales and Los Idolos. This proves the presence and power in

44 *Part of the Postclassic cemetery at Quiahuitzlan, with tombs in the shape of miniature shrines or temples.*

these places of foreign groups such as the Mexica.

Of the fortified towns, Tuzapan, situated in the Chicualote plateau, stands out due to its urbanized development with water tanks, drainage, sweat baths, and planned and paved streets.

The city of Cempoala impressed the Spanish invaders with its white-plastered walls and particularly its urbanism, including private and public services and well-developed cultivation techniques, based upon permanent irrigation systems, which caused the Spanish to remark 'all is green like a garden' (fig. 43). Its population was around 25 to 30,000 (Brüggemann 1987b; Brüggemann and Pereira 1987; Cortez 1986). Its main constructions were the Templo Mayor, the Temple of the Chimneys, the Temple of the Faces and the Divine Twins, and the so called 'House of Moctezuma', some of which show Mexica (Aztec) influence.

The cemetery of the Isla de Sacrificios, supposedly used for the burial of high-ranking individuals, was so named by the conquistadors after discovering freshly sacrificed corpses. A good

sample of pottery in the Isla de Sacrificios style has been recovered; decorated beautifully and with restraint, it shows a combination of geometric designs and naturalistic figures. An important collection of pieces from this site is held in the British Museum and comes from excavations carried out by Evan Nepean (col. pl. 28). Systematic work was undertaken by Celia Nuttall (1910), Miguel Angel Fernández, Wilfrido Du Solier (1938) and Alfonso Medellín Zenil (1955), and recently a brief salvage operation was carried out by Marina Alvarez and Sergio Vásquez.

Another important Postclassic site which should be mentioned is Quiahuiztlan, a centre that served as a military fort, ceremonial centre and cemetery (fig. 44), and was witness to the arrival of the Spanish invaders who founded the town of Villarica. More than eighty of its graves have been investigated. These resemble miniature shrines in which were placed the remains of the deceased accompanied by offerings, representations of the divinity and small zoomorphic sculptures thought to be a protector animal (Medellín 1951;

Navarrete 1984). Besides Quiahuiztlan, Texuc, Palma Sola and La Antigua, other tombs of this type (only partially excavated) have been found at some twenty sites.

Recently the University of Veracruz reinitiated excavations at Quiahuiztlan, restoring some of its main buildings. Work was carried out on sixteen structures, an intensive survey of the area was undertaken and the nuclear parts, the north and west cemetery, were mapped (Arellanos, Sánchez *et al.* 1992).

The so-called Huastec culture is one of the least researched in recent times, despite the fact that it covered a large territory with sites in the sierra and its foothills. It also stretched as far as the coastal lowlands, therefore including diverse ecological environments. This resulted in the development of different cultures, depending upon the resources available and the way in which they were exploited (Ortíz and Aquino 1978). This culture occupied parts of the states of Tamaulipas, San Luis Potosí, Querétaro, Hidalgo and some of northern Veracruz. Recently a team from the Instituto Nacional de Antropología e Historia (INAH), directed by García Cook and Merino Carrión, carried out work in the lower Pánuco River basin, which enabled them to establish a long cultural sequence beginning in the Early Formative and ending in the Postclassic. Despite not having the majesty of the Maya, its architectural style is unique (Du Solier 1945a).

The inhabitants of the Tabuco area, situated on the right bank of the River Tuxpan not far from the city of the same name, built structures with square, rectangular and horseshoe-shaped plans, and some with rounded corners. This city's occupation dates back to the Preclassic although its peak was in the Postclassic. It was invaded by the Tenochcas (Aztecs) in 1491 during the reign of Ahuízotl (Ortíz and Aquino 1987).

The Cacahuatengo area is on the plateau of the same name in Veracruz state and is thought to have been built around AD 1300. The city has well-constructed avenues, cisterns and wells for water supply, low circular shrines and large pyramid-shaped monuments, of which the 'Castillo' stands out, comprising seven main parts with rounded corners. This structure is surrounded on three sides by a *coatepantli* (serpent-wall) of stepped battlements. To date this area has not been investigated (Ekholm 1953; Medellín 1983).

Outside the city of Tuxpan in Veracruz is the Castillo de Teayo, excavated and restored by García Payón (1950, 1976a, 1976b), who believes that it was built and inhabited by the Toltecs. Only the main pyramid is left which is made up of three parts and has a total height of 11.2 metres. At its summit is the remains of a small shrine. A considerable number of worked sandstone sculptures also come from this site.

Situated in the state of Hidalgo, the Huejutla locality is important for being the first place where tombs form perfectly conceived architectural elements, separated from temples or public monuments. The floor consisted of a large sandstone monolith and walls were made from courses of stones kept in place with mud and worked on their internal faces. These supported the roof which was made from four large rocks weighing between 1 and 18 tons (Du Solier, in García Payón 1976b: 95).

Tamuín in San Luis Potosí is an important settlement covering approximately 17 hectares, although only one platform has been excavated. This structure was decorated with paintings that have almost all disappeared and that are the first and only ones found to date in the Huastec zone.

Huastec architecture is not as impressive as that seen in other areas of Mesoamerica such as El Tajín, Teotihuacan, Chichén Itzá and Palenque, but the Huastecs excelled in the craft of carved shell, bone and stone. The sculpture, whilst severe and static, can be considered as one of the most beautiful in Mesoamerica for its unique characteristics and profuse representations, displaying a style closely related to Tula and Chichén Itzá. The artistic predecessors of this style can be seen in the graceful clay figurines that were so common in the Preclassic period, although these show different concepts. One of the most outstanding and well-known pieces of sculpture is the 'Adolescent of Tamuín', which some have interpreted as Quetzalcóatl and others as a young man taking part in *Tepeílhuitl* celebrations linked to the Maize God, fertilization and rejuvenation (García Payón 1976a, 1979).

There are numerous sculptures of Tlazoltéotl, the goddess of 'filth' who cleanses man of his sins. Her cult was important for these people, as were the so-called 'lustful old men' who were related to the phallic cult, performed by the priests of this deity of agriculture, the moon and love. Huastec stelae also show detailed representations of priests doing penance.

No doubt because of the rivalry between the two ethnic groups, the Aztecs poured insults and abuse on this Huastec town in an attempt to disparage its far-reaching cultural achievements. The Spanish chroniclers followed this propaganda literally and describe the inhabitants as rough, sodomitic, drunken and lecherous.

Recent investigations in southern Veracruz: El Manatí, a sacred Olmec space

The El Manatí archaeological project began in 1988 with the chance discovery of an important mass offering by farmers from El Macayal. Whilst digging some tanks to be used for fish-farming they discovered the remains of an assemblage of wooden anthropomorphic sculptures (fig. 45), associated with objects never seen before in this region, such as rubber balls, human bone, seeds and other extremely well-preserved organic materials, as well as axes and pottery.

El Manatí is a salt dome situated in the south of Veracruz state in the lower River Coatzacoalcos basin. In the Municipio of Hidalgotitlán and on land belonging to El Macayal, it is one of the three highest points in the area. It is set in low-lying swamp land made up of archipelagos of small islands and lakes which join in places during the rainy season (it is probable that in ancient times

the area would have been permanently flooded). Fresh, clean water wells up from the foot of the eastern side of the hill of El Manatí, while on the west side are salt springs. In addition, the zone apparently has deposits of specular haematite, a valued red pigment.

More than 3,000 years before Christ, important religious ceremonies took place at this site. Ceremonies were performed over a long period of time by the people of one or several villages, culminating in the mass offerings of wooden sculptures accompanied by diverse materials, all well preserved due to the anaerobic conditions of a permanently flooded area.

According to radiocarbon dates, this sacred area was used from 1600 BC onwards over several centuries. The information recovered tells of activities linked to daily life, as well as special events that involved individual and collective social and economic effort.

In relation to these events, we can see that through time the nature of the offerings changed both in the type of objects deposited and the way in which they were arranged. The data obtained show that El Manatí was first occupied by a small permanent community or by temporary pilgrim campsites. The absence of a complete domestic complex, as seen in other domestic units, allows us to venture that the individuals who discarded these objects followed a specific diet, as the majority of the vessels are *tecomates*; globular, gourd-shaped vessels with narrow necks which are thought to have been used for boiling tubers and seeds, fermenting fruit and as containers. In addition to these are dishes with bevelled rims and vertical grooves. Another theory (with less support, although it cannot be rejected) is that these materials were brought and used by occasional pilgrims for food preparation and were then unintentionally discarded in the pond.

Regarding the function of the sculptures and associated objects, several hypotheses can be put forward. It would seem obvious that they were related to the water cult and its association with springs, the hill itself, and the rest of its contextual environment – forest, lakes and perhaps even a cave that has yet to be discovered at the foot of the hill or on its slope. As noted earlier, the hill of El Manatí is saline and salt water springs well up on its western side.

Judging by their finish it is possible that the sculptures had a specific function in an important ritual before their interment. Their individuality also suggests that they may have served as representations of chiefs, leaders or people who had attained some kind of high ranking, their images immortalized through the wooden carvings. The knives and staffs found in association with some of these images could be symbols of the power that the particular individual had in life.

There does not appear to be a definite pattern in the position of the burials. However, there is a consistency in the orientation of the ensemble, with three east–west axes leading towards the hill.

Bundles of leaves, plants and reed stalks fulfilled

45 *One of the wooden busts from El Manatí. It is carved in pure Olmec style and may have played a part in rituals connected with a water cult before its eventual interment.*

an important role in the magico-religious ceremony surrounding the burial of the wooden sculptures. It would appear that the busts received special treatment similar to that given to humans, as they were wrapped in reeds to form a bundle and were then deposited in a careful and sophisticated ritual.

The reason for choosing El Manatí as a sacred place possibly has to do with the fact that there are a number of elements associated with Olmec religious ideology. The springs flowing from the hill at one time formed a pool into which were thrown axes, jade beads and vessels, primarily *tecomates*. (There is another similar votive deposit, with axes and stone masks, at Arroyo Pesquero in Veracruz.) The haematite deposits could be another reason. On the other hand, its location at the western foot of a prominent hill also fits with examples seen at Chalcatzingo in Morelos state or Teopantecuanitlán in Guerrero, where the communities settled west of a prominent elevation in the area.

The data apparently indicates that the offerings were part of a single event that took place at one point in time, though as yet we cannot rule out the possibility that the site was subsequently used over several centuries and that what we have noted relates to just one of several ritual events.

Another point worth emphasizing is the presence of primary burials with scattered bones, including small femurs and skulls, associated with some of the sculptures; originally thought to belong to monkeys, these were therefore interpreted as accompanying offerings in the form of a *tona*. However, physical anthropologists have recently identified the bones as human, belonging to newborn foetuses. This revelation has completely changed previously held notions and brings a new level of complexity to this cultural phenomenon. We are now faced with possible evidence of child sacrifice and perhaps that of women who died during childbirth, or who had their foetuses removed whilst alive, perhaps even in some form of ritual cannibalism. It is evident

from the smaller sculptures (the stelae and altars) that children played a fundamental role in Olmec religious ideology. Their earliest significance is unclear, but in later periods they can be seen associated with the Rain God cult. We also know from the historical sources that during more recent times child sacrifice was common practice, especially amongst the Tenochcas, and was directly associated with water and fertility cults. The recent discoveries at the Great Temple in Tenochtitlan attest to these beliefs (see López Luján in this volume).

The data from El Manatí allows us to trace certain concepts that would later become an important part of the religious ideology of Classic and Postclassic peoples right up until the Conquest, according to the sixteenth-century historical writers and recent archaeological excavations.

Using an analogical approach, with all the risks that this implies, what follows are some ideas which are obviously open to debate. What is present at El Manatí is clearly a reflection of an important ceremony of which there remains only some paraphernalia in the form of a few cult objects. We will perhaps never know more about the prayers, songs, music, food and drinks that would have been part of the ritual.

What remains is an assemblage of artefacts that undoubtedly had a semiotic presence and are a reflection of this sacred event; they are signs or icons loaded with symbolism. However, how do we go about interpreting them if we lack substantial knowledge concerning social, political, and economic organization, which is precisely that which gives body to these expressions? But it is clear that these are evidence of an event linked to cults of nature, particularly water in the form of springs and the hills as elements that attract clouds and rain. Perhaps they are also related to the ancestors whose images are carved in wood, as seen in the relief 1-A of Chalcatzingo.

Again as an analogy, it is possible that the sculptures carrying batons are Tláloc's assistants, the *tlaloques, chaneques* or dwarves who live in the hills and springs and who control or bring on the vital element of rain by striking the clouds to release it. This could be depicted on Stelae 2 and 3 at La Venta. People carrying staffs are also represented on later stelae, but the batons have been interpreted as symbols of rulership. If so, as discussed earlier, these must then be images of leaders.

The cult and sacrifice of children in ceremonies associated with water and fertility lasted right up until the Conquest. It was believed that infants caused it to rain with their weeping, and we know they occupied an important place in Olmec representations. Because of this, some scholars have proposed that these 'child gods', born in the mountains, hills and caves, were symbolic of the origin myths. As Joralemon speculates, it is perhaps one of these ceremonies where the Rain God is brought back to the human world. Such rituals, he says, 'would have marked the beginning of the rainy season and were surely accompanied by the sacrifice of infants and small children'. Axes of green stones, such as jade or serpentine, also would have symbolized raindrops and crystalline waters reflecting the greenness of the vegetation and the sea.

In southern Veracruz, on the archipelago where El Manatí and other Olmec zones are situated and on the island of La Venta in Tabasco, scarcity of water is not the problem. Perhaps it was the sweet, fresh spring water in comparison to the undrinkable water of the permanent marshland that made the natural pools sacred places.

What then was the purpose of a ceremony laden with objects relating to the cults of fertility, water and hills? Was it perhaps to obtain, or plead for, clemency against the constant inundations and abundance of water? Perhaps events such as those that took place in Tuxtla after the eruption of San Martín and its secondary peaks also had repercussions in this area, leading to population movements, fires, deforestation and climate changes resulting in droughts, decrease in soil productivity and other disasters forcing them to make ritual offerings. Of course, there are still many aspects that need to be assessed, but for the present the abundance of water and its potential threat seem to be the most critical factors, requiring ceremonies to beg the gods for mercy.

In conclusion, the offering at El Manatí implies an elaborate ceremony possibly with the participation of several communities. It is difficult to understand a motive that could drive people to carry out a ritual requiring the burial of dozens of wooden sculptures, jade and serpentine axes, and the interment of people, animals and other sacred objects. The offering surely goes beyond the mere need for propitiatory rituals. It must relate to an exceptional event. Whatever it may have been, the ritual had a large number of participants and magic objects. It was carefully planned and executed. The result is extremely interesting, not only for the type of material present and its artistic quality, but because a careful analysis of the context containing the offerings, and the site as a whole, will allow a more extensive study into the magico-religious thoughts of Olmec communities, their beliefs, gods, mythology and other little-known aspects of this enigmatic culture.

References

Arellanos Melgarejo, Ramón (1985) 'Las Higueras –
Acacalco, dinámica cultural de un sitio en el
Totonacapan Barloventino'. Master's thesis. Xalapa:
Facultad de Antropología de la UV.

Arellanos Melgarejo, Ramón (1995) *La arquitectura
Postclásica de Quiahuiztlan: Estudio monográfico.*
Archivo Técnico del IAUV.

Arellanos Melgarejo, Ramón and Lourdes Beauregard
(1981) 'Dos Palmas Totonacas, reciente hallazgo en
Banderilla Ver.', *La Palabra y el Hombre*, Nos 38–9,
144–60. Xalapa: Universidad Veracruzana.

Arellanos Melgarejo, Ramón, Luis Sánchez, Lourdes
Aquino, Omar Alor, Lourdes Beauregard, Alfredo
Sánchez, José A. Sánchez and Francisco Vega (1992)
*Informe Preliminar de campo. Proyecto
Quiahuiztlan. Temporada 1992.* Archivo Técnico del
IAUV.

Bernal, Ignacio (1975) '*Los Olmecas*', *Del Nomadismo
a los Centros Ceremoniales*, 183–234. México:
SEP–INAH.

Brüggemann, Jürgen K. (1987a) 'Análisis urbano de El
Tajín', *El Proyecto Tajín. Cuadernos de trabajo de
Monumentos Prehispánicos*, No. 5. México: INAH.

Brüggemann, Jürgen K. (1987b) 'El estudio de los
objetos muebles en Cempoala', *Cempoala una
Ciudad Prehispánica.* México: Coleccíon Científica,
INAH.

Brüggemann, Jürgen K. and Armando Pereira (1987)
'Un conjunto urbano en la ciudad de Cempoala',
Cempoala una Ciudad Prehispánica. México:
Colección Científica, INAH.

Brüggemann, Jürgen K., Sara Ladrón and Juan Sánchez
Bonilla (1992) *Tajín.* México: Edit. El Equilibrista
S.A. de C.V. Citybank.

Caso, Alfonso (1942) 'Definición y extensión del
complejo Olmeca', *Mayas y Olmecas*, 43–6.
Sociedad Mexicana de Antropología. Chiapas:
Tuxtla Gutiérrez.

Ceja, Tenorio Fausto (1985) 'Paso de la Amada: An
Early Preclassic Site in Soconusco, Chiapas, México',
*Papers of the New World Archaeological
Foundation*, 49. Utah: Provo.

Clark, John E. (1989) 'Los orígenes de la civilización
olmeca: Los olmecas y Mocaya del Soconusco de
Chiapas, México', *El Preclásico o Formativo.
Avances y Perspectivas. Seminario de Arqueología
"Dr Román Piña Chan"*, 385–403. México: INAH.

Coe, Michael D. (1968) *America's First Civilisation:
Discovering the Olmec.* New York: The Smithsonian
Library, American Heritage Publishing Co.

Coe, Michael D. and Richard A. Diehl (1980) *In the
Land of the Olmec.* Austin: University of Texas
Press.

Cortez H., Jaime (1986) 'La hidráulica Urbana de la
Cempoala Prehispánica'. Tesis de licenciatura.
Xalapa: Facultad de Antropología de la UV.

Covarrubias, Miguel (1942) 'Origen y desarrollo del
estado artístico Olmeca', *Mayas y Olmecas. Segunda
reunión de la Sociedad Mexicana de Antropología.*
Chiapas: Tuxtla Gutiérrez.

Covarrubias, Miguel (1946) 'El arte Olmeca o de La
Venta', *Cuadernos Americanos* V, XXVII, 153–79.

Covarrubias, Miguel (1956) *The Eagle, the Jaguar and
the Serpent. Indian Art of the Americas.* New York:
Knopf.

Cyphers, Ann (1995a) *Descifrando los Misterios de la
Cultura Olmeca: Una exposición muesográfica de
los resultados del Proyecto arqueológico San
Lorenzo Tenochtitlan 1990–1994.* México: UNAM.

Cyphers, Ann (1995b) 'San Lorenzo Tenochtitlan', *Los
Olmecas en Mesoamérica*, John E. Clark (ed.),
43–68. México: Citybank, Editorial El Equilibrista.

Daneels, Annick (1988) 'La cerámica de Plaza de Toros
y Colonia Ejidal. Informe sobre las excavaciones
realizadas en el marco del proyecto "Exploraciones
en el Centro de Veracruz"'. Thesis. Editorial México.

Drucker, Philip (1943a) 'Ceramic stratigraphy at Cerro
de Las Mesas, Veracruz, México', *Bureau of
American Ethnology, Bulletin 141.* Washington DC:
Smithsonian Institution.

Drucker, Philip (1943b) 'Ceramic sequences at Tres
Zapotes', *Bureau of American Ethnology, Bulletin
140.* Washington DC: Smithsonian Institution

Drucker, Philip (1952a) 'Ceramic stratigraphy at La
Venta', *Bureau of American Ethnology, Bulletin 154.*
Washington DC: Smithsonian Institution.

Drucker, Philip (1952b) 'La Venta, Tabasco: A Study of
Olmec ceramics and art', *Bureau of American
Ethnology, Bulletin 155.* Washington DC:
Smithsonian Institution.

Drucker, Philip, R.F. Heizer and R.J. Squier (1959)
'Excavation at La Venta, Tabasco, 1955', *Bureau of
American Ethnology, Bulletin 170.* Washington DC:
Smithsonian Institution.

Du Solier, Wilfrido (1938) 'Isla de Sacrificios (entierros)', *Revista de Educación*. México.

Du Solier, Wilfrido (1945a) 'Estudio arquitectónico de los edificios huastecas'. *Anales del Instituto Nacional de Antropología e Historia*, 121–46.

Du Solier, Wilfrido (1945b) 'La cerámica arqueológica de El Tajín'. *Anales del Instituto Nacional de Antropología, Historia y Etnografía*, 5a época, 3, 2–45.

Ekholm, Gordon F. (1944) 'Excavations at Tampico and Pánuco in the Huasteca, México', *Anthropological Papers of the American Museum of Natural History*, 38, 321–509.

Ekholm, Gordon F. (1953) 'Notas arqueológicas sobre el Valle de Tuxpan y áreas circunvecinas', *Huastecos, Totonacos y sus vecinos*, 413–21. México.

Ekholm, Susanna M. (1968) 'Mound 30a and the early Preclassic Ceramic Sequence of Izapa, Chiapas, México', *Papers of the New World Archaeological Foundation*, 25. Utah: Provo.

García Payón, José (1942) 'Interpretación cultural de la zona arqueológica de El Tajín', *Mayas y Olmecas. Segunda Reunión de la Sociedad Mexicana de Antropología*. Chiapas: Tuxtla Gutiérrez.

García Payón, José (1950) 'Castillo de Teayo: noticias sobre su arqueología', *UNIVER T.* II, 16, 155–64. Xalapa.

García Payón, José (1951) 'La pirámide de El Tajín: estudio analítico', *Cuadernos Americanos* X, 6, 153–77. México.

García Payón, José (1952) 'El Tajín: trabajos de conservación realizados en 1951', *Anales del Instituto Nacional de Antropología e Historia* 23, 74–90. México.

García Payón, José (1966) 'Prehistoria de Mesoamérica: Excavaciones en Trapiche y Chalahuite, 1942, 1951, y 1959', *Cuadernos de la Facultad de Filosofía, Letras y Ciencias* 31. Xalapa: Universidad Veracruzana.

García Payón, José (1966b) 'Prehistoria de Mesoamérica', *Cuadernos de la Facultad de Filosofía, Letras y Ciencias*. Xalapa: Universidad Veracruzana.

García Payón, José (1971) 'Archaeology of central Veracruz', *Handbook of Middle American Indians* II, 505–42. Austin: University of Texas Press.

García Payón, José (1976a) 'Arqueología de la Huasteca. Consideraciones generales', *Los Pueblos y señoríos teocráticos; el periodo de las ciudades urbanas*, Segunda Parte, México, Panorama histórico y cultural VII, 58–122. México: SEP-INAH.

García Payón, José (1976b) 'La Huasteca', *Los señoríos y estados militaristas*, Panorama histórico y cultural IX, 243–90. México: SEP-INAH.

García Payón, José (1979) 'Quetzalcóatl', *Cuadernos Antropológicos del IAUV*, 2, 215–21, Xalapa.

Gillespie, Susan D. (1994) 'Llano de Jícaro: An Olmec monumental workshop', *Ancient Mesoamerica*, 5, 231–42.

Gonzáles Lauck, Rebeca (1995) 'La antigua ciudad Olmeca de La Venta, Tabasco', *Los Olmecas en Mesoamérica*, John E. Clark (ed.), 93-112. México: Citybank, Editorial El Equilibrista.

Grove, David C. (1981) 'Olmec Monuments: Mutilation as a clue to meaning', *The Olmec and their Neighbors, essays in memory of Matthew W. Stirling*, Elizabeth P. Benson (ed.), 48–68. Washington DC: Dumbarton Oaks.

Grove, David C. (1987) *Ancient Chalcatzingo*. Austin: University of Texas Press.

Grove, David C. (1994) 'La Isla Veracruz, 1991: A preliminary report, with comments on the Olmec uplands', *Ancient Mesoamerica*, 5, 223–30.

Joralemon, Peter David (1971) *A Study of Olmec Iconography*. Studies in Pre-Columbian Art and Archaeology 7. Washington DC: Dumbarton Oaks.

Justesen, John S. and Terrence Kaufman (1993) 'A decipherment of Epi-Olmec Hieroglyphic Writing', *Science*, 259.

Kampen, Michael E. (1972) *The Sculpture of El Tajín*. Gainesville: University of Florida Press.

Lira López, Yamile (1982) 'Un estudio estratigráfico en el sitio arqueológico de Chalahuite, Ver.' Tesis de Licenciatura. Xalapa: Facultad de Antropología de la UV.

Lowe, Gareth W. (1975) 'The Early Preclassic Barra Phase of Altamira, Chiapas: A Review with New Dates', *Papers of the New World Archaeological Foundation*, 38. Utah: Provo.

MacNeish, Richard S. (1954) 'An early archaeological site near Pánuco, Veracruz, México', *Transactions of the American Philosophical Society* 44, Part 5, 539–641.

MacNeish, Richard S. (1958) 'Preliminary archaeological investigations in the Sierra de Tamaulipas, México', *Transactions of the American Philosophical Society* 48, Part 6.

Martínez Donjuán, Guadalupe (1986) 'Teopantecuanitlán', *Arqueología y Etnohistoria del Estado de Guerrero*, 55–88. México: INAH-SEP-Gobierno del Estado de Guerrero.

Medellín Zenil, Alfonso (1951) *Exploraciones en Quiahuiztlan*. Xalapa: Archivo Técnico del IAUV.

Medellín Zenil, Alfonso (1953) *Exploraciones en los Cerros y Dicha Tuerta*. Xalapa: Archivo Técnico del IAUV.

Medellín Zenil, Alfonso (1955) *Exploración en la Isla de Sacrificios. Informe*. Xalapa: Gobierno del Estado de Veracruz.

Medellín Zenil, Alfonso (1960) *Cerámicas del Totonacapan: Exploraciones arqueológicas en el centro de Veracruz*. Xalapa: Gobierno del Estado de Veracruz.

Medellín Zenil, Alfonso (1975) 'Tribus y aldeas en el Centro de Veracruz', *Del Nomadismo a los Centros Ceremoniales*, Segunda parte, 9–57. México: SEP–INAH.

Medellín Zenil, Alfonso (1976) 'Las culturas del centro de Veracruz', *Los pueblos y señoríos teocráticos: El periodo de las ciudades urbanas*, Segunda parte, 9–57. México: SEP–INAH.

Medellín Zenil, Alfonso (1979) 'Clásico Tardío en el Centro de Veracruz', *Cuadernos Antropológicos del IAUV*, 2, 192–205. Xalapa.

Medellín Zenil, Alfonso (1983) *Exploraciones en la Región de Chicontepec o Huasteca Meridional (Temporada I 1955)*. Estado de Veracruz: Universidad Veracruzana.

Medellín Zenil, Alfonso (1987) *Nopiloa Exploraciones Arqueológicas 1957–1958*. Xalapa: Biblioteca, Universidad Veracruzana.

Navarrete, Mario H. (1984) 'La arqueología de la Antigua, Ver. (Epocas Prehispánicas y Colonial)'. Tesis de maestria. Xalapa: Facultad de Antropología de la UV.

Nuttall, Zelia (1910) 'The island of the sacrificios', *American Anthropologist* N.S. Vol.XII, 257–95.

Ortega, Jaime (1981) *Los entierros en El Zapotal*. Archivo técnico del IAUV.

Ortíz Ceballos, Ponciano (1975) 'La céramica de Los Tuxtlas'. Tesis de Maestría. Xalapa: T. I and II Facultad de Antropología de la Universidad Veracruzana.

Ortíz Ceballos, Ponciano and Lourdes Aquino (1978) *Tuxpan en la Huasteca: Un tratado de Imágenes*. Tuxpan, Ver., México: Banco de Tuxpan S.A.

Ortíz Ceballos, Ponciano and Lourdes Aquino (1987) 'Rescate arqueológico en Tabuco, Tuxpan, Ver.', *Boletín Informativo del IAUV* 6 Extraordinario, Xalapa.

Ortíz Ceballos, Ponciano, and Ramón Arellanos (1986) 'Delimitación de las zonas arqueológicas en el Centro de Veracruz', *Simposium La arqueología de Superficie, Veracruz 1983. Sociedad Mexicana de Antropología*. México: INAH.

Ortíz Ceballos, Ponciano, and Ma. del Carmen Rodríguez M. (1995) 'Los espacios sagrados olmecas: El Manatí un caso especial', *Los Olmecas en Mesoamérica*, John E. Clark (ed.), 69–93. México: Citybank.

Ortíz Ceballos, Ponciano and Robert Santley (1988) *La Cerámica de Matacapan. Monografía*. Archives of IAUV and Universidad de Nuevo México, INAH.

Santley, Robert S. and Ponciano Ortíz Ceballos (1985), Reporte Final de Campo, Proyecto Matacapán, Temporada 1983, *Cuadernos del Museo. Universidad Veracruzana* 4, 3–97. Xalapa.

Santley, Robert S., Ponciano Ortíz C. and Christopher A. Pool (1987) 'Recent archaeological research at Matacapán, Veracruz: A summary of the results of the 1982–6 field season in México', *Mexicon 9 (2)*, 41–8.

Stark, Barbara L. (1986) 'Informe Técnico parcial al Instituto nacional de Antropología e Historia del proyecto Arqueológico La Mixtequilla 1986', in the Archivo Técnico de la Dirección de Arqueología del INAH, México.

Stark, Barbara L. (1989) 'Patarata Pottery: Classic Period Ceramics of the South-Central Gulf Coast, Veracruz, México', *Anthropological Papers of the University of Arizona* 51.

Stuart, George E. (1993) 'The carved Stela from La Mojarra, Veracruz, México', *Science* 259, 1700–1702.

Stirling, Matthew W. (1943) 'Stone Monuments of southern México', *Bureau of American Ethnology, Bulletin 138*. Washington DC: Smithsonian Institution.

Stirling, Matthew W. (1965) 'Monumental sculpture of southern Veracruz and Tabasco', *Handbook of Middle American Indians* 3, 716–38. Austin: University of Texas Press.

Torres Guzmán, Manuel (1970) 'Exploraciones en la Mixtequilla'. Tesis de Maestría. Xalapa: Facultad de Antroplogía de la UV.

Torres Guzmán, Manuel (1972) 'Hallazgos en El Zapotal Informe preliminar (Segunda temporada)', *Boletín del INAH*, Epoca II, 3–8. México.

Valenzuela, Juan (1945a), 'La segunda temporada de exploraciones en la región de los Tuxtlas, Veracruz', *Anales del Instituto Nacional de Antropología e Historia*. T.I. México.

Valenzuela, Juan (1945b) 'Las exploraciones efectuadas en Los Tuxtlas, Veracruz', *Anales del Museo Nacional de México*, T. III, 5a época, 83–107. México.

Wilkerson, S. Jeffrey (1970) 'Un yugo in situ de la región del Tajín', *Boletín del INAH*, 41, September. México.

Wilkerson, S. Jeffrey (1972) 'Ethnogenesis of the Huastecs and Totonacs: early cultures of North Central Veracruz at Santa Luisa, Mexico'. Ph.D. Dissertation. New Orleans: Tulane University.

Wilkerson, S. Jeffrey (1980) 'Man's eighty centuries in Veracruz', *National Geographic Magazine*, 158 (2), 202–31.

Wilkerson, S. Jeffrey (1981) 'The Northern Olmec and Pre-Olmec Frontier on the Gulf Coast', *The Olmec and their neighbors: Essays in memory of Matthew W. Stirling*, 181–94. Washington DC: Dumbarton Oaks.

Wilkerson, S. Jeffrey (1987) *El Tajín: Una guía para visitantes*. Xalapa: Museo de Antropología de Xalapa y Ayuntamiento de Papantla, Veracruz.

7. Observations on the Late Classic Interregnum at Yaxchilán

Nikolai Grube

With its beautiful carved monuments the ancient Maya city of Yaxchilán has long fascinated scholars and laymen alike. The majority of the finely carved lintels and stelae were sculpted by artists who worked for only two of the many known rulers of the royal dynasty of Yaxchilán. These rulers, who commissioned almost all the architecture and sculpture visible at the site, were first identified by Tatiana Proskouriakoff in a groundbreaking study of Yaxchilán's history (1963, 1964). Since then, further research by Peter Mathews (1988), Carolyn Tate (1992), Linda Schele and David Freidel (1990), Werner Nahm (1997) and others has led to the reconstruction of a long list of kings, beginning with 'Penis Jaguar', who founded the dynasty around AD 320, and ending with K'inich Tab Kimi, the last known ruler, for whom the last recorded date is AD 808. While the sequence of rulers at Yaxchilán for the most part is remarkably complete, all scholars agree that the ten year 'interregnum' period between the death of Itzam Balam II ('Shield Jaguar') (figs 46c, d) in AD 742 and the accession of Yaxun Balam IV ('Bird Jaguar') (figs 46e, f) in AD 752 has remained opaque. Why did no successor accede to the throne of Yaxchilán on the death of Itzam Balam II? Why was the interregnum so long, longer than any other transitional period between the reigns of two rulers?

The most ambitious attempt to explain the long interregnum was undertaken by Linda Schele and David Freidel (1990: 262–305). They assume that a dynastic struggle arose because of rival claims to power caused by the fact that the actual successor,

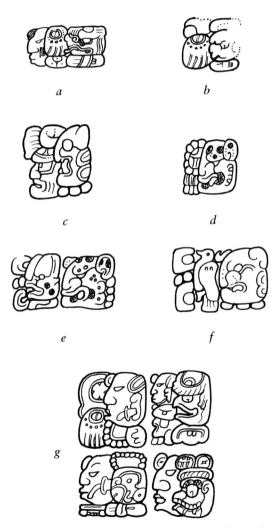

a   *b*

c   *d*

e   *f*

g

46 *The nominal glyphs of Lady K'abal Xok (a), the caught Yaxchilán lord (b), Itzam Balam II (c, d), Yaxun Balam IV (e, f), and 'Lady Eveningstar' (g). Note the Calakmul emblem glyph in the name of 'Lady Eveningstar'.*

Yaxun Balam IV, was the son of a foreign female and not of Itzam Balam's presumed first wife, Lady K'abal Xok (fig. 46a). They argue that there was also a conflict in which the local élite was involved because Lady K'abal Xok was from a local family while the mother of the heir, 'Lady Eveningstar' (fig. 46g), presumably came from the distant and powerful city of Calakmul. After Yaxun Balam IV finally came to power at 9.16.1.0.0 (29 April 752), he started an unprecedented propaganda campaign at Yaxchilán in which he attempted to legitimize his power and to strengthen the prestige of his mother. This campaign included his sculptural programme through which he created a retrospective history of Yaxchilán: he connected himself with the ancestors of the Yaxchilán lineage; he set his mother in scene together with his father; he downplayed the role of Lady K'abal Xok; and he claimed to have inherited rulership directly from his progenitor.

Evidence for the capture of the heir

New light has been shed on the interregnum since it was realized that on Step II of Hieroglyphic Stairway 3 from Dos Pilas (fig. 47) the event of a capture of a Yaxchilán *ahaw* – a ruler from Yaxchilán – is recorded (Hopkins and Josserand, personal communication, 1995; Houston 1993: 117). The step shows a bound captive lying on the

ground in a very uncomfortable position, his earrings torn out and replaced by paper strips as a sign of humiliation. The Calendar Round date of the event is heavily eroded. Other than the day sign Men and the coefficient 18 of the Haab, no further information is available to securely place the date in the chronology. However, Hieroglyphic Stairway 3 was built under the auspices of Dos Pilas Ruler 4 who acceded at 9.15.9.17.17 (23 June 741) and who is last mentioned at 9.16.9.15.3 (15 January 761). If the date of the capture is within the reign of Ruler 4, it could have been within the interregnum at Yaxchilán. Josserand and Hopkins argue that the interregnum was caused because the successor to the rulership fell prey to Ruler 4. They also observe that the name of the captive contains the *xok* glyph (fig. 46b), which is also part of the name of Lady K'abal Xok. They conclude that the captive was the son of Lady K'abal Xok and that he was the legitimate successor. His capture, they say, led to the long interregnum and finally to the ascendancy of Yaxun Balam IV.

In a hitherto unpublished note Héctor Escobedo has deciphered the date of the capture event on Step II. He recognized that the inscription begins with a Distance Number of 10 Winal and 12 days, which seems to connect the capture of the Yaxchilán heir with a capture event recorded on

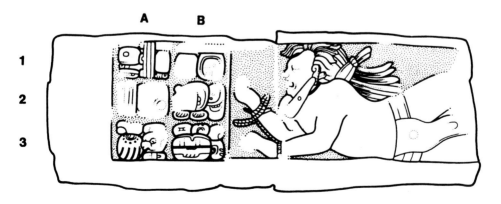

47 *Dos Pilas Hieroglyphic Stairway 3, Step II: the capture of a Yaxchilán* ahaw *at 9.15.13.15.15 (745).* (Drawing by Stephen D. Houston)

the unpublished Step IV. According to Escobedo, the capture of the Yaxchilán heir took place at 9.15.13.15.15 (745), three years after the death of Itzam Balam II, at Yaxchilán.

No epigraphic evidence exists at Yaxchilán of a ruler between Itzam Balam II and Yaxun Balam IV. Certainly, if another ruler acceded shortly after Itzam Balam's death at 9.15.10.17.14 (15 June 742), he remained in office for only three years at

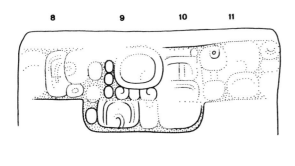

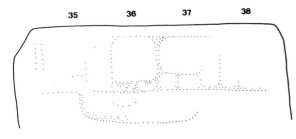

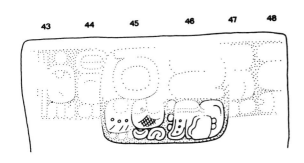

48 *Selected blocks from Yaxchilán Hieroglyphic Stairway I. These blocks show a later hieroglyphic text from the time of Yaxun Balam IV carved over previous cartouches. Step V, Hieroglyph 6, bottom (here the lowest block), is a reference to an* ox ahal eb, *'three victories stairway'. (After Graham 1982: 143–51)*

the most, until falling prey to Dos Pilas Ruler 4. If he had his own monuments recording his accession, these were certainly removed or destroyed either during the attack by Dos Pilas or as a consequence of Yaxun Balam's rewriting of the history.

Although there is no direct clue, Hieroglyphic Stairway 1 at Yaxchilán could have been a monument originally erected by the ruler who acceded after Itzam Balam's death (fig. 48). It is clear that the stairway has been recarved. The original inscription consisted of at least eighteen, and probably twenty, large carved cartouches. The later inscription was commissioned by Yaxun Balam IV and records the 'official history' of Yaxchilán, beginning with the founder of the dynasty and concluding with Yaxun Balam IV himself (Mathews 1988: 89; Nahm 1997). Although Graham (1982: 141) considers the possibility that the cartouches were added after the hieroglyphic inscription had been carved, a close inspection of both the drawings and the photos seems to support Mathews' conclusion that the cartouches, which contained human portraits as well as texts, were carved first. It is of particular interest to note that the cartouche on Step V, under Hieroglyphs 45 and 46, contains a reference to *ox ahal eb*, 'the stairway of the three victories', a common designation for stairways built after successful conquests (Freidel, Schele and Parker 1993: 353–5).[1] If the cartouche texts were written during the interregnum, the question arises whether they were commissioned by the Ruler of Dos Pilas to commemorate his victory over Yaxchilán (much like the Naranjo Hieroglyphic Stairway which records the conquest by Caracol, and the Seibal Hieroglyphic Stairway which records the victory by Dos Pilas) or whether they were written by the 'interregnum ruler' to record his first success in warfare. Whatever was written on the Hieroglyphic Stairway originally, it fell victim to Yaxun Balam's ambitious programme to undo all traces of earlier history that would cast doubt on his legitimacy.

The question of the political motivation for the capture

The capture of the successor to the throne must have been a dramatic incident in the history of Yaxchilán. Why did Ruler 4 of Dos Pilas attack Yaxchilán? What was the motivation behind the capture? There is no evidence that Dos Pilas greatly profited from the capture of the Yaxchilán king. Nor can we recognize any evidence at Dos Pilas of increased wealth or an expanded sphere of influence under the reign of Ruler 4. Whatever happened, for the people at Dos Pilas the capture of the Yaxchilán lord was the climax of the conflict between the two centres and the only aspect of the aggression which was regarded as important enough to be recorded. The capture of the Yaxchilán lord by Dos Pilas is in some way similar to the capture of Waxaklahun Ubah K'awil, the 13th Ruler of Copán, by K'ak' Tiliw, the ruler of Quiriguá, in that the capture of the king did not result in the destruction of the site. However, at Copán, only forty-three days after the capture of Waxaklahun Ubah K'awil, a new ruler acceded to the throne. He probably was not a very powerful king, but at least dynastic succession was secured. At Yaxchilán, the process of re-establishing rulership was delayed for several years.

In this essay I will try to reconstruct the political scenario which may have provided the background and rationale for the elimination of the 'interregnum ruler' at Yaxchilán. One possible reason could have been the political ambitions of more powerful patron states. The rulers of Dos Pilas explicitly stated that they were vassals (*y-ahaw*) of a much larger state whose emblem glyph consisted of a snake (*kan*) sign, which has been identified in the past with the huge city of Calakmul (Marcus 1976; Martin 1994). Dos Pilas, however, was not the only state to acknowledge the superior power of Calakmul. Rulers of many other lowland Maya states, such as those from Naranjo, Caracol, El Perú, Cancuén and, though less obvious, Piedras Negras, also referred to themselves as the clients of the lords of Calakmul

(Martin and Grube 1995, 1996; Grube 1994). Calakmul was one of the most influential political powers in the Maya lowlands, but not the only one. Because of their size and the richness of their architecture, cities such as Palenque, Copán and the highland site of Toniná have been long seen as dominant forces in their region. The most populous and influential kingdoms, however, were located in the Petén, where Calakmul and Tikal controlled antagonistic groupings of states (Martin and Grube 1995, 1996). It is still a matter of debate whether the cities along the Usumacinta river were part of the political spheres existent in the Petén or whether they conformed to a different pattern and were largely independent from the superpowers operating further north. In the Petén most of the warfare originated from tensions between Tikal, Calakmul and their particular allies. Could the capture of the Yaxchilán heir have been motivated by similar antagonisms?

Yaxchilán is one of the few cities in the Maya lowlands where none of the recognized signs of subordination is found, which could be interpreted as an indication that the city managed to stay neutral. However, one should be cautious in interpreting Yaxchilán in this way. It is possible, if not likely, that Yaxun Balam IV considered any evidence for a subordinate position of the Yaxchilán state to be humiliating and that he destroyed any earlier evidence that may have existed.

Alliances of states along the Usumacinta River

Even though, at first glance, Yaxchilán appears to have remained largely outside of the major hegemonic spheres, other cities along the Usumacinta river did not. A little further down the river lies the city of Altar de Sacrificios. David Stuart and Stephen Houston have found evidence that Altar de Sacrificios maintained some kind of diplomatic ties with Tikal; Altar de Sacrificios's Stela 8 mentions the 22nd ruler of Tikal at 9.9.15.0.0 in a passage which is not yet clearly understood.

The fact that the city of El Chorro, situated halfway between Altar de Sacrificios and Yaxchilán, was also the target of a Dos Pilas attack – as recorded on Step I of Dos Pilas Hieroglyphic Stairway 3 (Houston 1993: 117–19) – shows that antago-nistic relations must have existed between the two. Whether this also implies that both cities pertained to different hegemonic spheres – Dos Pilas to that of Calakmul and El Chorro to that of Tikal – is a hypothesis that should be studied further because it has implications both for the political motivation of Maya warfare as well as for the interpretation of the position of Yaxchilán.

Further downstream along the Usumacinta river is situated the big city of Piedras Negras. Piedras Negras controlled several 'provincial capitals' such as El Cayo, La Mar and for some time also Bonampak and Lacanhá. It was a powerful city which very early in its history had successfully extended its sphere of influence through warfare. Early monuments from Piedras Negras such as Panel 2 record the presentation of captives from surrounding polities, including Yaxchilán. One of the captives on Panel 12, the earliest-known monument from Piedras Negras, can be identified through the hieroglyphic caption as the Knot-Eye-Jaguar, the ninth ruler of Yaxchilán (Mathews 1988: 76). Unfortunately, however, there are no further monuments from the Early Classic at Piedras Negras which would help to resolve the question of whether the capture of Knot-Eye-Jaguar resulted in a durable integration of Yaxchilán into the Piedras Negras sphere or whether there were no further traces left at Yaxchilán of the capture of its king. The fact that shortly after the capture a new king acceded, the tenth ruler of Yaxchilán, suggests that Piedras Negras never completely integrated Yaxchilán into its state. However, we may also consider that there were very subtle grades of integration and political control exerted by Piedras Negras on Yaxchilán which have not been preserved in the epigraphic record.

That Piedras Negras continued to exert considerable influence on Yaxchilán even more than a hundred years later is suggested by Panel 2, dated 9.11.15.0.0 (AD 667) (fig. 49). Panel 2 shows six warriors kneeling before Piedras Negras Ruler

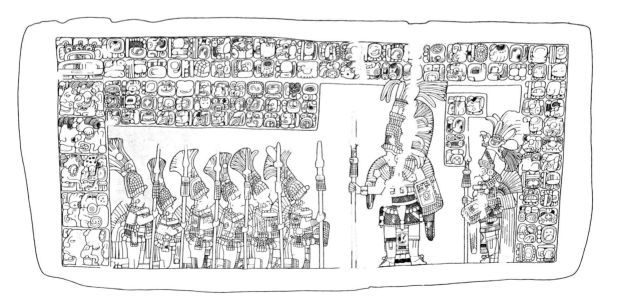

49 *Piedras Negras Panel 2.* (Drawing by David Stuart)

2 and his heir to the throne. The small hieroglyphic captions over their heads identify them as lords from three other important polities in the area: Lacanhá, Bonampak and Yaxchilán. It is the fifth warrior in front of the Piedras Negras ruler who through his emblem glyph can be identified as an *ahaw* (lord) of Yaxchilán. At the same time, there is a hiatus of monuments at Yaxchilán, a further sign that its rulers were not granted the right to erect their own monuments (Miller, n.d.).

The iconographic and epigraphic record at Piedras Negras suggests that its rulers held a number of states, including Yaxchilán, in somewhat unruly submission. The question arises whether Piedras Negras was integrated into even larger hierarchies, as defined by the political spheres of Tikal and Calakmul.

Even though the rulers of Piedras Negras only reluctantly recorded their integration into a higher political order, four clues have been found which place Piedras Negras within the hegemonic sphere of Calakmul. On Panel 12, the early Ruler 'Fishfin' states that he is a *y-ahaw* 'vassal' of another king, whose name is not spelled out, but who uses the 'west *kalomte*' title which occurs only once more at Piedras Negras in association with the ruler of Calakmul. On Panel 2, in a retrospective passage dealing with the same Ruler 'Fishfin', he is recorded having received his war helmet *y-ichnal* 'in the company of' Tahom Uk'ab Tun, west *kalomte*'. This is the nominal phrase of one of the early rulers of Calakmul (Martin and Grube, forthcoming), and this particular event, the gift of a war helmet, was so important that it was commemorated in many later inscriptions. Piedras Negras Ruler 2 records an unknown event on Stela 35 which involves a lord from Calakmul. Finally, on a small looted panel from the Piedras Negras region, the adorning of the leather helmet of Piedras Negras Ruler 2 by either a Calakmul ruler or a high subsidiary lord from Calakmul is commemorated. All of this suggests that Piedras Negras was not beyond Calakmul's influence.

The role of Piedras Negras in the accession of Yaxun Balam

Dos Pilas and Piedras Negras were the political powers which were influential before and during the interregnum at Yaxchilán. Rulers of both cities had intense connections with Calakmul and were in subordinate positions to it. It is possible that besides their alliance they had also shared common political interests. Yaxchilán is situated halfway between Dos Pilas and Piedras Negras, and a loyal ruler there must have been in the interest of both. An antagonistic ruler could have blocked vital communication and trade routes along the Usumacinta river.

Although it would be purely speculative to claim that Dos Pilas and Piedras Negras had co-ordinated their strategy against Yaxchilán, hieroglyphic texts at Piedras Negras suggest that the re-establishment of a new and friendly king was planned and executed at Piedras Negras. Only five years after the capture of the original Yaxchilán heir by Dos Pilas at 9.15.13.15.15 (AD 745), Piedras Negras Ruler 4 celebrated his first K'atun (twenty years) in office. According to the long inscription on Piedras Negras Panel 3 (fig. 50), this event was celebrated there in the company of a 'divine lord of Yaxchilán'. The Yaxchilán ruler carried a variant of the dynasty founder's name, which it is possible is a pre-accession name of Yaxun Balam IV, but it could also have been another otherwise unrepresented ruler during the interregnum who wanted to make clear that he was a true successor to the founder. In any case, this Yaxchilán lord 'came to witness in the canoe' and took part in the K'atun festivities, which included a 'descending macaw dance' of the Piedras Negras Ruler and a night-time banquet that included 'drinking of fermented [?] cacao'.

A similar royal visit, in which a foreign ruler comes to witness the accession of his host, is recorded just one other time in Maya inscriptions. This is Dos Pilas Panel 7, a monument describing the visit of Dos Pilas Ruler I at Calakmul for the

50 *Piedras Negras Panel 3.* (Drawing by Linda Schele)

accession of Jaguar Paw the Great at 9.12.13.17.7, or 3 April 686 (Houston 1993: Figure 5.11). Since in this case it is the vassal who attends the accession of his new patron, we might also wonder whether the visit recorded on Lintel 3 expresses a sort of hierarchy with the Yaxchilán ruler being the weaker of the two.

The date 9.16.1.0.0 (29 April 752) marks the official accession of Yaxun Balam IV at Yaxchilán. At this point the interregnum definitely came to an end. The accession also initiates the onset of an unprecedented building program by which Yaxun Balam IV changed the appearance of the entire city. By that time he was already forty-two years old and therefore older than most other rulers by the time of their accession. While other, younger rulers usually erected their first monuments many years after their accession, Yaxun Balam IV must have acquired enough power and authority during the interregnum to start his ambitious monument programme immediately. Whether he had this authority because of his advanced age or whether

it was because he was backed by Piedras Negras will be difficult to ascertain.

That Piedras Negras was a major force behind Yaxun Balam IV finds direct support in further texts from Panel 3. A small incised text to the left of the throne mentions an event which took place at 9.16.6.10.19 (8 November 757) and whose agent was Yaxun Balam IV. Although the text has not yet been deciphered, the same event is probably recorded on Yaxchilán Lintel 12 (fig. 51), which carries a date only one day later. Here Yaxun Balam IV appears with four captives and a subordinate lord, suggesting that the event recorded in the incised text of Panel 3 was also related to warfare.

The small text continues with a Distance Number of 23 days and leads to another event. The verbal phrase is *hok'ah ti ahawle* 'he came out into kingship', followed by the name of Yaxun Balam IV and an agency phrase which records that the accession took place under the auspices of a certain individual named 'Turtleshell' (fig. 52).

51 *Yaxchilán Lintel 12.* (After Graham and von Euw 1977: 33)

52 *A passage from the incised hieroglyphic text of Piedras Negras Panel 3. The first four glyphs read* hok'ah ti ahawle yaxun balam, *'He came out as king, Yaxun Balam'. The fifth glyph is the agency expression* u kahi *or* u ch'abhi, *'by the doing of', and the last glyph is the name of a Piedras Negras lord, 'Turtleshell'.*

The 'Turtleshell' hieroglyph is part of many, if not all, names of Piedras Negras rulers. However, we cannot define Ruler 4 as the agent of this accession statement. The text on Panel 3 provides the information that Piedras Negras Ruler 4 died at 9.16.6.11.17 (26 November 757), only eighteen days after the war event, so that it is possible that he participated in a battle together with Yaxun Balam IV. Unlike Yaxun Balam IV, however, who seems to have been successful, Ruler 4 might have been wounded and died. His burial took place three days after his death, and Yaxun Balam's accession is recorded in the incised text as two days later.

The individual under whose auspices Yaxun Balam's accession took place, 'Turtleshell', could have been the heir to the Piedras Negras throne or one of its aspirants. The name of the next king, Ruler 5, is different. Ruler 5 acceded only at 9.16.6.17.1, about four months after the aforementioned events. The 'Turtleshell' hieroglyph could either have been his pre-accession name or, alternatively, a patronymic title. In any case, these events shed light on the nature of relations between Yaxchilán and Piedras Negras in the early years of Yaxun Balam's reign. It seems that Yaxun Balam IV was a close ally of Ruler 4, both because of his presence during the K'atun anniversary and their participation in the same battle. When Ruler 4 died, Piedras Negras saw a short interregnum of four months followed by the accession of the relatively weak Ruler 5. Ruler 5 was regarded as so unimportant that Ruler 7, the last documented ruler of Piedras Negras, avoided mentioning him on Panel 3. The death of Ruler 4 must have represented a sudden decline of the former power of Piedras Negras. It was only at this point that Yaxun Balam's accession, which had taken place six years previously, was acknowledged at Piedras Negras. The fact that the accession was still recorded as being 'under the auspices of' an individual from Piedras Negras supports the conclusion that Yaxun Balam IV was sponsored by Piedras Negras, even though for

obvious reasons of self-esteem he failed to acknowledge the superiority of Piedras Negras on his own monuments.

Under the reign of the rather weak Ruler 5 the fate of the two cities seems to have changed. While Piedras Negras's power declined, Yaxun Balam IV led his city to its greatest florescence. It appears as if Yaxchilán for the first time was really free from its ever dominating neighbour downstream.

Conclusion

In this essay I have developed the hypothesis that the replacement of the original Yaxchilán heir by Yaxun Balam IV was part of a concerted strategy of the two cities Dos Pilas and Piedras Negras. While Dos Pilas caught the ruler who had acceded to the throne upon Itzam Balam's death, Piedras Negras's role was to take care of Yaxun Balam IV as the next successor, a successor whose mother 'Lady Eveningstar' was a royal female from Calakmul, the patron state to which the client states Dos Pilas and Piedras Negras belonged. The reason why the 'interregnum ruler' at Yaxchilán was eliminated may have been his rapprochement to another political sphere, that of Tikal. One should remember that the next largest polities further south, El Chorro and Altar de Sacrificios, may also have maintained ties to Tikal.

There is no direct evidence for contacts between the 'interregnum ruler' and states within the Tikal sphere. However, I tentatively suggest that the emancipation of Yaxchilán from the Piedras Negras domination, which started under the reign of Itzam Balam II, may have been possible only through the support of a powerful state which did not belong to the same hegemony as Piedras Negras itself. In a similar strategy Quiriguá looked for powerful backing from Calakmul when it freed itself from Copán (Looper 1995), and Caracol was supported by Calakmul against Tikal (Grube 1994). It seems that wherever there was a strong regional power controlling subordinate cities the process of liberation almost necessarily involved the establishment of alliances with the antagonistic superpower. States in the Tikal sphere strived for alliances with Calakmul and vice versa.

That this process had already begun during the reign of Itzam Balam II[2] is suggested by the small caption associated with the small prisoner on the lower right of Piedras Negras Stela 8 (fig. 53). The caption says that at 9.14.14.9.18 (AD 726)[3] a captive was taken whose name was *u-?*. The captive was a sublord (*sahal*) of 'the guardian of Ah Nik' and was taken by Yonal Ak, the predecessor of Ruler 4. The title phrase, *u chanul ah nik*, 'the guardian of Ah Nik', is always associated with Itzam Balam II, and that the phrase refers to Itzam Balam II as the overlord of the captive is strongly supported by a heavily eroded Yaxchilán emblem glyph which follows it. The Piedras Negras ruler Yonal Ak thus had taken a captive who was a sublord of Itzam Balam II, which is clear evidence that the relations between the two cities under Itzam Balam II had changed to open conflict. It is interesting to note that Itzam Balam's building programme starts at about the same time as the capture date, providing further evidence that he strived to free Yaxchilán from foreign dominion.

One of the mysteries that remains to be solved is the origin and identity of Yaxun Balam's mother, 'Lady Eveningstar'. According to her nominal phrase on Yaxchilán Stela 13, she is from Calakmul. One wonders how Itzam Balam II could have a wife from Calakmul and still strive to become an ally of Tikal. However it may be significant that 'Lady Eveningstar' is only recorded retrospectively on sculptures commissioned by her son, Yaxun Balam IV. What was her original status during the life of Itzam Balam II? The only evidence we have about her may well have been made up by her son as part of his grand programme to legitimate his political position. Whether she was indeed from Calakmul or whether marriage patterns do not always conform to political alliances – a possibility which seems unlikely but will still have to be considered – should be the focus of future research.

53 *The captive at the lower right on Piedras Negras Stela 8 and the accompanying hieroglyphic caption (greatly enlarged). The hieroglyphic text reads '4 K'an 17 Sotz' (9.10.7.7.4), 14 days, 2 Winal, 7 Tun and 4 K'atun later it came to pass 5 Etz'nab 16 Sip (9.14.14.9.18) when it was caught u-? the sublord of the guardian of Ah Nik, Yachilán ahaw, by the doing of Yonal Ak, 4 K'atun ahaw'. (Drawing by Nikolai Grube)*

The 'interregnum ruler' probably only continued or culminated a process of separation which was initiated by Itzam Balam II. I hypothesize that Yaxchilán's break from its former patron was the underlying political motivation for Calakmul's client states Dos Pilas and Piedras Negras to remove the Yaxchilán king.

If the reconstructed political scenario proves true, the 'interregnum episode' at Yaxchilán would be one more case for an attempted political volte-face which was not met with success. Another such case is represented by the Naranjo ruler who succeeded Ruler I in office. While Ruler I acceded under the auspices of the king of Calakmul (Martin and Grube 1996), the next ruler changed to hostility and, as recorded on Step VI of the Hieroglyphic Stairway from Naranjo, met his end as a result of a 'Star War' at 9.9.17.11.14 (1 October 630), after which he was probably taken captive and tortured (*k'uxah*) at Calakmul (Martin 1991: 26–31). These examples suggest that the ultimate sanction against secession was military might and that coercive threat was a factor in maintaining political spheres. Calakmul and its vassals seem to have been much more successful defenders of their political spheres than Tikal, which in the early Late Classic period had lost the majority of its former clients to Calakmul. Although there is no support for the claim that all political activity in the southern lowlands conforms to a 'grand strategy', there is increasing evidence that such activity in the Usumacinta area was at least heavily influenced by the same large-scale alignments which operated in the central area.

Notes

1. The *ox ahal eb* reference on Yaxchilán Hieroglyphic Stairway 1 and its possible implications were first explained to me by Werner Nahm in 1995.

2. More evidence for a political rapprochement of Itzam Balam II to Tikal was gained during an inspection of Maudslay's plaster casts of the Palenque Hieroglyphic Stairway in the British Museum by Linda Schele, Peter Mathews and myself in the summer of 1996. Even though the syntax of the hieroglyphic text still remains a mystery, the inscription mentions an Itzam Balam, *ahaw* of Yaxchilán at 9.11.6.16.11 7 Chuen 4 Ch'en (7 August 659). It is possible that this Itzam Balam is Itzam Balam II at the rather tender age of about eleven years (given that his birth, as Proskouriakoff (1963) has calculated, had taken place some time around 9.10.15.0.0). The three last hieroglyphs of the same phrase mention Ruler 'Shield Skull' of Tikal. Of the two glyphs between the Yaxchilán emblem glyph and the 'Shield Skull' name, the second is the same 'Imix variant' glyph which is also found between the name of K'ak' Tiliw of Quiriguá and the name of a Calakmul lord on Quiriguá Stela I. At Quiriguá this glyph represents some kind of diplomatic tie or friendly relation to Calakmul. I suppose that this glyph represents the same type of relation on the Palenque Hieroglyphic Stairway, but between Yaxchilán and Tikal.

3. Because of the faintness of the incision, reconstructing the chronology for the capture event has proved to be difficult. However, the photo published by Maler (1901: Plate XVII) shows enough detail to permit decipherment of the dates. The capture event took place at a date 5 Etz'nab 16 (month glyph). A distance number of 4.8.2.14 leads from this date back to a previous date, which cannot be seen in Maler's photo, but can in drawings by Morley (1937–8: Plate 31), where it is clearly 4 K'an 17 Sotz'. Since the agent of the capture is given as Yonal Ak, the only possible Long Count placement for the capture is 9.14.14.9.18, a date which falls at the end of Yonal Ak's reign. The earlier date is 9.10.6.7.4 4 K'an 17 Sotz' and falls within a few days after the accession of Ruler 2, Yonal Ak's father. Unfortunately, the nature of the earlier event is not known.

References

Freidel, David, Linda Schele and Joy Parker (1993) *Maya Cosmos. Three Thousand Years on the Shaman's Path*. New York: William Morrow.

Graham, Ian (1982) *Corpus of Maya Hieroglyphic Inscriptions, Vol. 3, Part 3: Yaxchilán*. Cambridge, Massachusetts: Peabody Museum of Archaeology and Ethnology, Harvard University.

Graham, Ian and Eric von Euw (1977) *Corpus of Maya Hieroglyphic Inscriptions, Vol. 3, Part 1: Yaxchilán*. Cambridge, Massachusetts: Peabody Museum of Archaeology and Ethnology, Harvard University.

Grube, Nikolai (1994) 'Epigraphic research at Caracol, Belize', *Studies in the Archaeology of Caracol, Belize*, Diane Z. Chase and Arlen F. Chase (eds), 83-122. Monograph 7. San Francisco: Pre-Columbian Art Research Institute

Grube, Nikolai (1996) 'Palenque in the Maya World', *Eighth Palenque Round Table, 1993*, Merle Greene Robertson, Martha Macri and Jan McHargue (eds), 1–13. The Palenque Round Table Series, Volume 10. San Francisco: The Pre-Columbian Art Research Institute.

Houston, Stephen D. (1993) *Hieroglyphs and History at Dos Pilas. Dynastic Polities of the Classic Maya*. Austin: University of Texas Press.

Looper, Matthew (1995) 'The Sculpture Programs of Butz' Tiliw, an Eighth-Century Maya King of Quiriguá, Guatemala'. Ph.D. Dissertation. Austin: Department of Art and Art History, University of Texas.

Maler, Teobert (1901) *Researches in the Central Portion of the Usumatsintla Valley*. Memoirs of the Peabody Museum of American Archaeology and Ethnology, Vol. II, No. 1. Cambridge, Massachussetts: Harvard University.

Marcus, Joyce (1976) *Emblem and State in the Classic Maya Lowlands*. Washington DC: Dumbarton Oaks.

Martin, Simon (1991) 'Some Thoughts and Work-in-Progress'. Unpublished manuscript. London.

Martin, Simon (1994) 'Calakmul en el Record Epigráficas: Informe Preliminar'. Manuscript to be published in the First Report of the Proyecto Arqueológico de la Biosfera de Calakmul, Ramón Carrasco V (ed.). Mérida, Yuc.: INAH.

Martin, Simon and Nikolai Grube (1995) 'Maya Superstates. How a few powerful kingdoms vied for control of the Maya Lowlands during the Classic period (AD 300-900)', *Archaeology* 48(6): 41–6.

Martin, Simon and Nikolai Grube (1996) 'Evidence for Macro-Political Organization of Classic Maya States'. Manuscript on file. Washington DC: University of Bonn and Dumbarton Oaks.

Martin, Simon and Nikolai Grube (forthcoming) *Chronicle of the Maya Kings*. London: Thames and Hudson.

Mathews, Peter L. (1988) 'The Sculpture of Yaxchilán'. Unpublished Ph.D. Dissertation. Dept. of Anthropology, Yale University.

Miller, Mary Ellen (n.d.) 'Relations between Yaxchilán and Piedras Negras'. Manuscript to be published in Research Reports on Ancient Maya Writing. Washington DC: Center for Maya Research.

Morley, Sylvanus G. (1937–8) *The Inscriptions of Petén*. 5 vols. Washington DC: Carnegie Institution of Washington, Pub. 437.

Proskouriakoff, Tatiana (1963) 'Historical Data in the Inscriptions of Yaxchilán, Part I', *Estudios de Cultura Maya 3*: 149 67. México: UNAM.

Proskouriakoff, Tatiana (1964) 'Historical Data in the Inscriptions of Yaxchilán, Part II', *Estudios de Cultura Maya 4*: 177–201. México: UNAM.

Schele, Linda and David Freidel (1990) *A Forest of Kings*. New York: William Morrow.

Tate, Carolyn E. (1992) *Yaxchilán: The Design of a Maya Ceremonial City*. Austin: University of Texas Press.